DEBRETT'S
SALMON STORIES

DEBRETT'S
SALMON STORIES

By
JACK CHANCE

Illustrations by
Fred Banbery

Foreword by
His Grace the Duke of Devonshire
M.C., P.C.

DEBRETT'S PEERAGE
LIMITED

Text Copyright © Jack Chance 1983
Illustrations Copyright © Fred Banbery 1983
Published by Debrett's Peerage Limited,
73-77 Britannia Road, London S.W. 6.
First published 1983
All Rights Reserved
ISBN 0 905649 61 3
Designed by Addy Pritchard
Typeset by Capital Letters London W1
Printed in Great Britain by
The Garden City Press Limited
Letchworth, Hertfordshire SG6 1JS

"The Salmon is a gentle fish, but he is cumbrous to take; for commonly he is but in deep places of great rivers, and commonly in the middlest of the rivers."

("A Booke of Fishinge with Hooke and Line" by Mascall, 1590)

But you wouldn't think so by the behaviour of some of them as revealed here.

ACKNOWLEDGEMENTS

His Grace The Duke of Devonshire M.C., P.C.
for his introduction and authority for publication of the Billie Flynn stories.

Viscount Coke
for his kindness in allowing access to the Holkham Hall fishing records and permission to publish excerpts. Also, to Lady Sylvia Combe and Lady Mary Harvey for allowing the use of photographs taken on the Alta by their father, the Earl of Leicester.

David Hopley
for providing me liberally with stories from his salmon-fishing library.

The Editor of *The Field*
for authority to use excerpts from my articles which have appeared in his columns.

The Editor of *Country Life*
for the use of Miss Beamish's remarkable story ***The One that Got Away*** which first appeared in ***Country Life*** in 1955.

Chapman and Hall
for permission to reproduce the Bromley Davenport epic.

Hutchinson & Co.
publishers of ***Three Salmon at a Speyside Funeral*** by Col. Andrew Haggard.

The Director of the Salmon and Trout Association
and the Editor of its magazine.

J.M. Dent & Sons
for the use of an incident described by Lady Evelyn Cotterell in ***Salmon Fishing on the Spey***.

The President, Secretary and Librarian of the Fly-fishers Club
for unrestricted access to their magnificent library.

J.W.C.

CONTENTS

CHAPTER FOUR
ELATION

FOREWORD

I am proud to have been asked to write a foreword to Jack Chance's highly entertaining little book of "Salmon Stories" and am delighted that he has rescued from oblivion some of the great fishermen and women of the past, and, indeed, the records of some famous catches. But I am well aware that the reason I have been accorded this honour is not so much on account of my own prowess with rod and line as on account of our mutual friendship with the late Billie Flynn.

I am now 63 and I can say with my hand on my heart that many of the happiest days of my life have been spent salmon fishing on the River Blackwater in County Cork in the Republic of Ireland, and many of these happy times I spent in the company of Billie Flynn. It is difficult to describe him, but the best I can do is to call him a "stage" Irishman. Like many of his countrymen, he preferred good manners to the truth. This had the advantage of making him the most delightful company; at the same time one realized that it would be unwise to believe a word he was saying.

Fortunately he died at the reasonable age of 73 in 1964. I use the word "fortunately" advisedly, since later in the year a great tragedy took place on the river when three of his ghillies were drowned when their boat overturned. This would have been more than Billie could bear. A further but lesser misfortune was to follow, which was that in the autumn of the same year the dreaded salmon disease broke out, from which the river has never fully recovered.

My friendship with Billie was one of the happiest things that has happened to me in my singularly fortunate life and I am delighted that some of his tales are included in this book. He was a man in a million.

Devonshire
Chatsworth House
1983

INTRODUCTION

Accounts of dramatic encounters with Atlantic salmon over nearly two centuries are so well documented in a plethora of fishing books as to have become stale news to salmon fishermen in every country where the sport is pursued. A good example is the world record catch on the Grimersta (Hebrides) in August, 1888, in freak conditions never likely to be repeated, as related by Augustus Grimble. Likewise, many splendid stories by other writers of the last century spring to mind: Stoddart, Cornwallis-West, Gathorne-Hardy, Calderwood, "B.B.", Shaw, Scrope, Knox, George Browne, Courtney-Williams, Malloch, Hardy, Bickerdyke, Francis Francis, Jardine, to name but a few. They tell of fabulous adventures with monster fish and will ever be revered by anglers everywhere. Some are true, others legendary. In this book the author has relied upon less familiar data, although some of the stories have appeared in ephemeral sporting magazines and some in books now rare and long out of print. They are offered in the manner by which the chronicler of Sherlock Holmes inevitably introduced each successive display of the master's magical powers. In other words, they seemed to me to expound *some feature of particular interest*. Had Sir Arthur Conan Doyle been a fisherman, you may be certain that Holmes and Watson would have found themselves in situations at least as inhospitable and intimidating as Dartmoor and the Reichenbach Falls (not salmon water of merit). Exposed to the perils of Norwegian fosses, Canadian rapids and Scottish ghillies of former days, they could have survived only by the supreme exercise of the master's intellect on one of his better days. An ancillary hazard would have been the devious plots laid for their destruction by the versatile Professor Moriarty.

I fancy that Moriarty would have been the more skilled angler, with his infinite resource and patience extending over at least a century and four or five volumes, than Holmes with his partiality for opium, the violin and making Scotland Yard look ridiculous. Attributes not, you will agree, essential to aspirants for an honours degree in fly-fishing.

Now we must address ourselves to the exacting task of telling the reader about the problems which have for many years confronted the salmon fisherman and, of course, the salmon.

J.W.C.

CHAPTER ONE
SUCCESS

SUCCESS

We start with a mixed bag of formidable salmon fishermen and women – and what an unlikely bunch they are! It would surely have taxed the ingenuity of a Wilkie Collins or an Agatha Christie to have conjured up a plot in which an Irish ghillie, a French chef, a portly English nanny, a Herefordshire alderman and the richest Duke in the world all had a role. But here they all are, each enjoying their relative measure of success. The records of their achievements, though soundly documented at the time, are no longer readily available and needed bringing to light; and this is what we have done.

——————1——————

THE HOLKHAM RECORDS

A T Holkham Hall in Norfolk there is a remarkable record of salmon fishing in the Arctic Circle of Norway, never before publicly disclosed and never, one can safely assert, to be surpassed. The leather-bound book modestly inscribed "ALTEN NORWAY" contains details with photographs of the capture of Atlantic Salmon by the Duke of Westminster ("Bendor") and his friends from 1913 to 1929. One of them, Viscount Coke, later the 4th Earl of Leicester, preserved these records with scrupulous attention to detail. Authority to quote from them and to reproduce certain entries and photographs has been generously granted by the present Viscount Coke.

You will not find much in books about the Alta

River which, about 30 miles long, flows northwards at lat. 70° x long. 23°. The Alta and the Tana are the two most northerly rivers in Europe. In its peak years the Alta was largely the preserve of two Dukes, Westminster and Roxburghe, for a few weeks in July. The Duke of Westminster and his guests normally arrived there in his private yacht. The guests included General Sir Redvers Buller, who had commanded the British Army in the Boer War, the Earl of Dalhousie, General Sir J. Laycock, Viscount Coke, Colonel North Dalrymple-Hamilton, Major B. Corbet and a few others.

The Alta has been owned for generations by some 200 smallholders who provided the boatmen and ghillies. That was the background to successive years of fantastic fishing, mainly on fly. But in 1965 a syndicate organized by Norway's largest travel agency, Mytravel International, became tenants of the whole river, after two years of negotiation with the owners, and built an impressive fishing lodge. Despite a weekly fee of £1,000 per rod, paid mainly by American sportsmen, the venture failed and was brought to an end after a few seasons of relatively meagre bags. No method could be found of controlling the poaching, despite the use of police patrols and helicopters from the NATO air-base.

Reverting to the great years, the catches were on a scale never to be attained on any Norwegian river except for the much shorter Bolstad near Bergen (named Vosso nowadays) where C.M. Wells, of whom more anon, achieved what no salmon fisherman had done before or since. Excerpts from the Holkham fishing book for July, 1923, record 372 salmon at an average of 21 lbs. The rods were Coke, Morrison, Corbet and Dalrymple-Hamilton. From 7 to 22 July, 1926, the catch was 684 by the Duke of Westminster, Laycock, Corbet and Dalrymple-

Hamilton, a record year. The best day's catch during the Duke's tenancy was on 1 July with 53 salmon weighing 1268 lbs and averaging 23.9 lbs. 1927 produced a mere 236 fish from the Duke of Roxburghe, Coke, Corbet and Dalrymple-Hamilton. 1928 improved to 462 of which fifteen exceeded 40 lbs and 82 of 30 lbs and over. The average weight was 24 lbs.

July in the Arctic Circle has no hours of darkness and on the nights of the 8th and 9th Coke and Dalrymple-Hamilton killed 35 fish averaging 28 lbs. But one of the most remarkable achievements, perhaps of all time, came on the night of 7 July at Upper Soutzo when the Duke of Westminster killed to his own rod 33 salmon weighing 800 lbs. The entry is reproduced on page 57 and shows that six exceeded 30 lbs and two 40 lbs. The strength and endurance of the Duke in a fast-running, turbulent river passes comprehension. It is unlikely that such a performance will be equalled in our time.

----------- 2 -----------

NANNY TO THE RESCUE

A family party from England had taken a fortnight's fishing on a small river, the Bandon, near the village of Tuosist in Southern Ireland. Three of them were experienced salmon fishermen but their diligence and persistence achieved nothing.

O N the evening before their departure, Nanny asked if she might have a go, since no fish had been caught. Permission granted, Nanny set off with a stout rod and a prawn, mounted for her by her employer, at the end of the line. She had never previously handled a rod. When she had not appeared to put the children to bed there was general concern. A slender wooden bridge in need of repair had to be crossed and nanny weighed fifteen stone.

The ghillie was sent to find her. He returned after a while carrying four salmon, followed by Nanny flushed with victory. On the following morning, the day of departure, she implored her mistress for a last attempt before breakfast. This request was reluctantly conceded and Nanny set off with her rod and a fresh prawn. She returned an hour later with two salmon, explaining that her technique was to pull them ashore as soon as they were hooked. This story goes to show that expertise counts for nothing in pursuit of salmon bent on suicide.

NANNY TO THE RESCUE

BACKWARDS DOWN THE FOSS!

On 9 July, 1968, when fishing the River Alta in Northern Norway as the guest of an American friend, an English lady hooked a fish at 3 am by the light of the midnight sun. She was using a yellow "Bucktail" tube fly and a 12-ft split-cane rod. The river was high, at 2 ft on the gauge, and the struggle which followed is worthy, in my view, of a detailed description.

S VARTFOSSNAKKEN pool lies just above the Svartfoss rapids, where boats must be hauled overland. Salmon lie at the head of the rapids where they are clearly seen as they rise to the fly. The boat is allowed to drift down the pool to the head of the rapids, a perilous operation in water rapidly gaining in speed and force. If a hooked fish chooses to descend the rapids, its chances of survival are almost certain, since, except in high water, a boat cannot follow.

On this momentous night the lady angler had two young, virile ghillies as oarsmen, both able to speak a little English.

After an hour's play in the pool, the fish moved into the main current and down the Svartfoss rapids it rushed. None of the older ghillies would have faced the boisterous descent which followed. Indeed, in living memory, the ordeal had only once been achieved. Instructed to lie down, the brave lady did so as the boat accelerated backwards down the white water with the outboard motor flat out and the oarsmen pulling as hard as they could against the current. She clearly recalls that her fear was alleviated slightly by her efforts to recover the backing on to her reel.

After 2¾ hours the fish was seen for the first time and came within reach of the gaff. At the first attempt the gaff broke and off went the salmon again.

Happily, because the return of the party to the lodge was by now several hours overdue, other ghillies were on the alert. A larger gaff was soon forthcoming and the prize was brought ashore at 6 am, 4½ miles downstream from the point at which it had been hooked.

It could not be weighed until the following after-noon because the lodge scales did not exceed 50 lbs. Luckily, the late Duke of Roxburghe, staying at the next Lodge downstream, was able to record a weight of 53 lbs. It was a cock fish, 52″ long and 29″ in girth. Scale tests showed it to be nine years old, four of which had been spent in the river and five at sea.

Its captor modestly attributes her success to her two young Norwegian ghillies, but for whose courage and skill this story might have ended in disaster.

4

THE WIZARD OF THE WYE

Robert Pashley, known as the Wizard of the Wye, lived at Walford, near Ross, and the following account of his achievements is taken from a book called **Wye Salmon and Other Fish** *by J. Arthur Hutton, published in 1949.*

THE actual number of salmon and grilse caught in the Wye by Robert Pashley are given below, and I am very glad to have this opportunity of publishing them, for I know of no other record like it, and the act of writing about it almost gives me a feeling of reflected glory. These figures also show what the Wye is capable of when fished by a really expert angler. I don't know who it was who gave him the well-deserved title of "The Wizard of the Wye".

YEAR	NO. CAUGHT	YEAR	NO. CAUGHT	YEAR	NO. CAUGHT	YEAR	NO. CAUGHT
1908	136	1918	105	1928	277	1938	103 E
1909	111 A	1919	166	1929	250	1939	367
1910	207	1920	160	1930	141	1940	226
1911	132	1921	140	1931	354	1941	319
1912	332	1922	193	1932	296	1942	257
1913	117	1923	194	1933	461	1943	370
1914	41 B	1924	163	1934	284	1944	291
1915	20 C	1925	222	1935	326	1945	312
1916	— D	1926	535	1936	678	1946	371
1917	— D	1927	138	1937	116	1947	211
	1096		2016		3183		2827

Total 9122, average weight about 15½ lb = 141, 391 lbs = 63 tons.

(a) Not complete.

(b) No late summer or autumn fishing.

(c) On odd days' leave.

(d) In Belgium, France and hospital, did not fish.

(e) Laid up with neuritis and did not fish in June and July.

The following are details of his three best seasons:

(1926) 535 fish weighing 7557½ lbs, average weight, 14.1 lbs, 404 with fly and 131 with bait. Every single fish was either gaffed or "tailed" by himself. The total rods-catch that season was 4033, so his catch amounted to 13½ per cent of all the fish caught in the whole of the river. I remember this wonderful catch very well, for there was a little controversy in the fishing papers as to whether it was the world's record catch of Atlantic Salmon for a single rod in one season. Curiously enough, in the same season Colonel Taylor also had a wonderful catch of 544 fish in the Tweed and Tyne, but this included some sea-trout, and the total weight was only 5520 lb. Probably, as far as numbers only are concerned, Pashley's catch was not a record, but, as far as I know, no one landed so large a weight of salmon and grilse in any one season.

His next great catch was in 1933 and 461 fish, 7740½ lbs, average weight 16.8 lbs, or 10½ per cent of the total catch in the whole river, namely 4019 fish.

However, these two great catches were not enough, and in 1936 he landed 678 fish, weighing 10,882 lbs, with an average weight of 16 lbs. The total rods-catch that season amounted to 5916, so again Pashley was responsible for over 10 per cent of the total. I feel quite quite sure that this marvellous catch, as far as weight is concerned and also possibly for numbers, is the world's record catch of Atlantic Salmon by a single rod in any one season.

It is rather remarkable that in two of the bumper seasons, 1913 and 1927, he caught only 117 and 138 fish. Even at Hampton Bishop we could show better figures for those two seasons, namely 291 and 206, but I must point out that there were usually two or three rods fishing our water. The total catches in those two seasons were 3354 and 6145. The explanation is that in those two years his opportunities for fishing were very limited. Most of his fishing has been in the Hill Court and Goodrich waters, two of the best beats in the Lower Wye, but in 1913 and also in 1927 they were let to other fishermen. It is quite a mistake to think that Pashley was always able to fish in both, or even in one, of those two lengths, and he never had the monopoly of them till 1938. They were frequently let to other rods, and in many seasons he could only fish there on one or possibly two days in each week, but when he did get the opportunity he generally made the most of it. I remember that in 1927 and 1928 he told me that he then had very little water available, and I then arranged with Sir John Mitchell (part-owner of the Hampton Bishop Fishery) for Pashley to come and fish whenever there was a vacancy, and our catches in those two years were thereby increased by 22 and 53 fish.

His records also show some wonderful one-day catches – on six occasions he had 10 fish in a day (102, 119½, 121, 132½, 144½, and 204 lbs), once 11 (120 lbs), three times 12 (111½, 143 and 166 lbs), once 14 (162 lbs), once 15 (174½ lbs), twice 16 (210 and 225 lbs) and once 18 (201½ lbs). The eighteen fish were caught on 20 September, 1932, all with fly. The total weight was 201½ lbs, giving an average of 11½ lbs, but the weight of the sixteen caught on 30 August, 1935, was 210 lbs, with an average weight of just over 13 lbs. These were all caught in the Vanstone when the water was dead low with fly and an ordinary trout-rod. The weights varied from 8½ up to 19 lbs.

The other sixteen were caught in 1936 and weighed 225 lbs, with an average of 14 lbs. Unfortunately he was dining out that evening and had to chuck it when the fish were still taking. I am afraid that if I had been in his place I should have been late for dinner. But I know that Pashley is a most conscientious chap, perhaps sometimes almost too much so.

He also has 29 "Portmanteaux" to his credit, ranging from 40 up to 48½ lbs. I wish he could have caught a 50-pounder, for if anyone deserves one he does. he is about the best "trier" I have ever met, and there is no doubt that the man who catches the most fish is the one whose line is "longest in the water". I had a good example of this in 1928. On April 6 I was lucky enough to catch eight fish weighing 166½ lbs, which was up to then our record one-day catch for weight, but not for numbers. In my opinion when dealing with record catches of salmon, weight should always count more than mere numbers. Later on in the month Pashley came over to give me a helping hand. On April 28 the river was rather on the low side and there was not a great deal of fishable water on our half of the beat, so in the morning I sent him up to the Carrots. I caught only one, 20½ lbs, down below, but he came in with four good fish, 19¼, 20½, 29 and 29½ lbs. As usual after lunch we changed beats, but before starting he asked me if I had seen many fish down below, and I told him nothing except the fish I had caught. He then suggested that he should go down to Lugg's Mouth, which meant a walk of one and a half miles there and the same coming back. It was a beast of an afternoon, bitterly cold north-west wind with occasional hail showers, so I begged him not to go as he was looking rather tired. However, he would go and he came back in the evening with three more fish, 22, 25 and 25½ lbs. This made his total seven fish

170½ lbs, our record one-day's catch for one rod. He was more than tired when he came in, but I was able to administer some restorative medicine at dinner-time. I was not so persevering and I did not stick it very long at the Carrots, which is very much exposed to the north-west wind, but I managed to catch one 35½ lbs, in the Carrots Hole. Only one was caught in the other half of the water making a total for the day of ten fish weighing 242 lbs. The following extract is from our diary:

"Very few fish seen – a real bitterly cold day. R.P. had a devil of a time with his last fish. The line got fast on the ledge. They sent a ring down but there was not enough current to float the line off, and, when he pulled to break, the line came away with the fish still on, and it was successfully landed. All this happened during a violent hail storm.

R.P. having broken J.A.H.'s record won't be invited again.

It is remarkable that so many fish were caught when so few fish were seen."

I say again that Pashley is a wonderful "trier", and he certainly deserves every fish he catches. Needless to say that he was invited again and added forty-five more fish that season to the Hampton Bishop catch.

Some people think that Pashley does nothing but fish. On the contrary, he is a very busy man and gives up a lot of time to public work. As I said before, he is troubled with a conscience, and is often working for other people when he might be fishing. Here are some of his numerous occupations – for forty years a member of the Ross and Whitchurch Rural District Council, elected to the Herefordshire County Council in 1919 and an Alderman in 1938, Member of the Wye Catchment Board, Chairman of the Parish

Council, twenty-nine years Hon. Treasurer of the Oddfellows and last, but not least, Chairman of the Wye Board of Conservators.

Unfortunately his heart got rather badly strained in the First World War, and I have always felt a little bit uneasy about his health. In 1937 he had to give up wading and, what was worse, he was no longer able to fish from the bank. But, in spite of this great handicap, he still managed to pull out a good many fish. I have often wondered how he managed to get through so much public work in addition to all his efforts to "empty the Wye." I am sorry to say that in his last letter he told me that he had given up the Dog Hole and the Vanstone, "as I can no longer do the water justice."

In conclusion let me say what a pleasure it has been to me to pay this tribute to my old friend "The Wizard of the Wye."

————— 5 —————

MR JAMESON'S 30-POUNDER

The Duke of Devonshire, in his Foreword, has paid a handsome tribute to the late Billie Flynn. My own tribute to the memory of a great fisherman and a great friend is the inclusion in this book, by way of light relief, of a few stories which Billie told me over the years, often several times and with many varia- tions, and which I committed to paper some time ago. Let us start with the story of how Billie brought Mr Willie Jameson's fishing career to a successful conclusion.

M ANY Careysville visitors will testify to the re-sourcefulness which Billie displayed from time to time. Others were the unwitting victims of his flair for a prank. Into this category we must place the late Mr Willie Jameson, joint tenant of Careysville for many years. Mr Jameson, having killed countless salmon on this beat, arrived at what was to be his last season without having achieved his life's ambition. This was to kill a fish of 30 lbs or more.

Fishing the Lane stream on a spring day he hooked a large fish which in the course of being played gave promise that his ambition would be achieved. Billie, however, was apprehensive about its weight when the fish was eventually landed. While Mr Jameson went off to the fishing hut to celebrate the event, Billie took the fish, under the pretext of weighing it, to the ghillie's quarters at the back of the hut.

A quick glance at the scale showed that it failed by a pound or so to make the coveted weight. Something must be done, and at once. The remains of lunch lay at hand. With the gaff handle used as a ram-rod, orange peel, banana skins, cheese and seed-cake were des-patched down the gullet until the target had been

MR JAMESON'S 30-POUNDER

reached. Then the fish, now scaling just over the 30 lb mark, was presented to an exultant Mr Jameson who, surveying the salmon's newly acquired *embonpoint*, exclaimed, "What a pretty fish!"

The sequel to this happy event came a week or so later when the fishmonger at Billingsgate market, in acknowledging the last consignment from Careysville, added a personal note to the letter. He felt bound, he wrote, to comment on one large salmon in particular, the contents of whose stomach revealed a catholic choice by any standards, and, for a fish, an unusual variety of fare. "All it needed," he added, "for its Christmas dinner was a bottle of champagne".

6

THE BEAUFORT CHEF

The Beauly River and its two tributaries, the Glass and the Farrar, are the property of Lord Lovat of Beaufort Castle, Inverness. The following story was told to me by Willie Matheson, for over fifty years head ghillie to Lord Lovat and his father. He was an eye-witness. I have heard that the fish may still be seen in a glass case at the Estate Office in Beauly.

THE French chef decided one evening to try his luck on this famous river. It was his first attempt at fishing with a fly and he chose to use it on the Kilmorack beat below the Stone Pool, not far from the Castle. Although he was unable to cast more than a few yards, a large salmon made off with the fly from the tangle of line. Being without experience, the playing and eventual landing took so long that the triumphant angler, after celebrating in the traditional

Highland manner, was unfit to attend to his culinary
duties that evening. The fish weighed 49 lbs, still the
record for the river.

THE BEAUFORT CHEF

CHAPTER TWO
DISTRESS

DISTRESS

Anyone who has fished, be it for perch, pike, trout, salmon, tarpon, mahseer or marlin, has endured the haunting experience of loss. Sometimes a loss which leaves a wound never quite healed by time or by a defective memory.

This collection of stories, two major and the others of less consequence, come from three Norwegian rivers, Rauma, Maals and Sand, and two Scottish rivers, Earn (Perthshire) and Awe (Argyllshire).

Two are tragedies in the literary styles of the 19th and 20th centuries and as contrasting as those of Euripides and Shakespeare. But both authors convey compassion for a noble foe, leaving the reader with admiration for fish and fisherman. I don't recall Macbeth or his lady being sorry about poor Duncan.

1

TRAGEDY ON
THE RAUMA

*I first read this story at the age of six, after my father had caught me reading **Dracula** by candlelight and had ordered a change of author. In this way my early ambition to become a vampire was converted into a passion for fishing. The account is taken from William Bromley Davenport's book **Sport**, published in 1888. In the morning he had landed a 43-pounder on the family beat on the Rauma in Southern Norway. We pick up the story at five o'clock on the afternoon of the same day.*

– 25 –

F IVE o'clock p.m. – we have eaten the best portion of a Norwegian sheep, not much bigger than a good hare, for our dinner, and the lower water awaits us. Here the valley is wider the pools larger and less violent. It is here that I have always wished to hook the real monster of the river – the sixty or seventy-pounder of tradition – as I can follow him to the sea if he don't yield sooner, which from the upper water I can't, because impossible rapids divide my upper and lower water, and if I had not killed this morning's fish where I did I should have lost him, as it was the last pool above the rapids. We take ship again in Nedre Fiva, a splendid pool, about a mile from my house, subject only to the objection which old Sir Hyde Parker, one of the early inventors of Norway fishing, used to bring against the whole country:– 'Too much water and too few fish!' I have great faith in myself today, and feel that great things are still in store for me. I recommence operations, and with some success, for I land a twelve and a sixteen pounder in a very short space of time; after which, towards the tail of this great pool, I hook something very heavy and strong, which runs out my line in one rush almost to the last turn of the reel before Ole can get way on the boat to follow him, and then springs out of the water a full yard high; this feat being performed some 120 yards off me, and the fish looking even at that distance enormous. I have no doubt that I have at last got fast to my ideal monster – the seventy-pounder of my dreams. Even the apathetic Ole grunts loudly his 'Gud bevarr!' of astonishment. I will spare the reader all the details of the struggle which ensues, and take him at once to the final scene, some two miles down below where I hooked him, and which has taken me about three hours to reach – a still back-water, into which I have with extraordinary luck contrived to guide him, dead-beat. No question now about his size.

We see him plainly close to us, a very porpoise. I can see that Ole is demoralised and unnerved at the sight of him. He had twice told me, during our long fight with him, that the forty-three pounder of this morning was 'like a small piece of this one,' – the largest salmon he had ever seen in his fifty years' experience; and to my horror I see him, after utterly neglecting one or two splendid chances, making hurried and feeble pokes at him with the gaff – with the only effect of frightening him by splashing the water about his nose. In a fever of agony I bring him once again within easy reach of the gaff, and regard him as my own. He is mine now! he *must* be! 'Now's your time, Ole – can't miss him! – now – now!' He does though! and in one instant a deadly sickness comes over me as the rod springs straight again, and the fly dangles useless in the air. The hold was broken! Still the fish is so beat that he lies there yet on his side. He knows not he is free! 'Quick, gaff him as he lies. Quick! do you hear? You can have him still!' Oh, for a Scotch gillie! Alas for the Norwegian immovable nature! Ole looks up at me with lack-lustre eyes, turns an enormous quid in his cheek, and does nothing. I cast down the useless rod, and dashing at him wrest the gaff from his hand, but it is too late. The huge fins begin to move gently, like a steamer's first motion of her paddles, and he disappears slowly into the deep! Yes–yes, he is gone! For a moment I glare at Ole with a bitter hatred. I should like to slay him where he stands, but have no weapon handy, and also doubt how far Norwegian law would justify the proceeding, great as is the provocation. But the fit passes, and a sorrow too deep for words gains possession of me, and I throw away the gaff and sit down, gazing in blank despair at the water. Is it possible? Is it not a hideous nightmare? But two minutes ago blessed beyond the lot of angling man – on the topmost pinnacle of angling fame! The practical possessor of the largest salmon ever taken with a rod! And now, deeper than ever plummet sounded, in the depths of dejection! Tears might relieve me; but my sorrow is too great, and I am doubtful how Ole might take it. I look at him again. The same utterly blank face, save a projection of unusual size in his cheek, which makes me conjecture that an additional quid has been secretly thrust in to supplement the one already in possession. He has said not a word since the catastrophe, but abundant expectoration testifies to the deep and tumultuous workings of his soul. I bear in mind that I am a man and a Christian, and I mutely offer him my flask. But, no; with a delicacy which does him honour, and touches me to the heart, he declines it; and with a deep sigh and in scarcely audible accents repeating – 'The largest salmon I ever saw in my life!' – picks up my rod and prepares to depart. Why am I not a Stoic, and treat this incident with contempt? Yes; but why am I human? Do what I will, the vision is still before my eyes. I hear the "never, never" can the chance recur again! Shut my eyes, stop my ears as I will, it is the same. If I had only known his actual weight! Had he but consented to be weighed and returned into the stream! How gladly would I now make that bargain with him! But the opportunity of even that compromise is past. It's intolerable. I don't believe the Stoics ever existed; if they did they must have suffered more than even I do in bottling up their miseries. They *did* feel; they *must* have felt – why pretend they didn't? Zeno is humbug! Anyhow, none of the sect ever lost a salmon like that! What! "A small sorrow? Only a fish!" Ah, try it yourself! An old lady, inconsolable for the loss of her dog, was once referred for an example of resignation to a mother who had lost her child, and she replied, "Oh, yes! but *children are not dogs*!" And I, in some sort, understand her. So, in silent gloom I follow Ole homewards.

THE ONE THAT
GOT AWAY

*The following account of an epic battle on the River Awe, in the Pass of Brander, Argyllshire, was published in **Country Life** in March, 1955, and deserves, as I hope you will agree, to be reprinted. It was written by Miss Huldine V. Beamish, who was at the time housekeeper to the "Old Man", whose name was Thornton. Awe fish were notoriously heavy in pre-Hydro days, but, as with all salmon rivers everywhere, the monsters have largely vanished or have been caught in nets in the sea or in estuaries.*

I AM going to call the angler in this story the Old Man. Some older sportsmen may remember him as the only angler of his time to catch two salmon weighing over 50 lbs in the British Isles. Both came from the River Awe in Argyllshire and I was in at the death of the second one. I was also present at the celebration of his thousandth salmon, a pretty good achievement for rod and line. But I want to tell you now of the one that got away, although no words can really describe the excitement and emotion of that red-letter day, when almost certainly the grandfather of them all cheated the gaff.

One morning, in hot summer, the Old Man left the bungalow he had built above the Seal Pool with rod and ghillie, saying he was going to fish downwards right from the top of the river. We arranged that in an hour or so I would also go to the top with a trout rod, and follow down after the salmon pools had been fished. I went on with my chores for about an hour, by which time the Old Man should have been in sight of the house. I looked up river and saw no sign of him.

This meant he must either have seen or caught a salmon. I got my rod and wandered upwards. The Black Pool above was deserted, and when I got on the road which ran just above the Shallows, I saw the Old Man playing a fish there; he was about half-way down this immense pool, standing on one of the piers. The fish appeared to be large, going deep and slow, and plenty of line was off the reel.

When I came up to him, the Old Man said he had already been there some time, as the fish had run straight out of the pool above after being hooked. He added that it was either a very big salmon or a smaller one foul-hooked, perhaps in the back. In any case, neither he nor the ghillie had at any time seen the fish, he was playing so deep. We did not have much time to talk, because almost at once the salmon started making for the tail of the pool in one long powerful rush. The Old Man put on all the strain he dared, and did everything he knew to stop the line running off the reel. Several times he succeeded, but no matter how much line he reeled in, the salmon never showed itself; the strong current cut past the line, which looked as if it had been anchored. By this time the struggle had been going on for nearly an hour. Several cars, some with fishermen going up to Loch Awe, had stopped, and their occupants had come down the bank to watch.

There was a prolonged singing of the reel, and the backing showed on the drum. The Old Man grunted, backed cautiously along the stone pier, and had to run down the rock-strewn shore as hard as he could go, reeling in and holding the rod high to keep the line away from the tops of the boulders showing in the rapids. The spectators followed along the top of the bank. In this way the Black Pool was reached; here at least would be a pause. The Old Man managed to mop his face with a handkerchief.

A long struggle took place in the Black Pool, where the fish became sulky, sinking for as long as ten to fifteen minutes into the extreme depths, but never showing any sign of weakening. The Old Man did all he could to keep him moving, and occasionally the ghillie and I were told to throw stones into the deep black water, hoping that would frighten him into movement. Of course, the longer a big fish can lie on the bottom, the more he recovers strength; it is only by making him fight without a pause that he can be weakened. By this time the Old Man had come to the conclusion that this must be a fair-sized specimen hooked elsewhere than in the mouth. The spectators increased until the bank was lined with them. At one moment a bus unloaded its passengers, but happily their timetable soon took them away again.

It looked as though there would never be an end to this plodding fight, but finally the salmon grew tired of the Black Pool, weary of his unsuccessful efforts to lie on the bottom, bored with persistent annoyances. Suddenly he came to life and – doubtless thinking of the freedom of the sea-loch that lay beyond this confining river – made a determined dash for the tail of the pool. The ghillie and I groaned. Surely he was not going out again! He was and he did, so fast that the Old Man had to run at the risk of falling over the stones. Down went the fish through the next set of rapids, never stopping, with all the line out and some of the backing, and the spectators running as well. We eventually reached the Seal Pool, and everything appeared to be intact. The Old Man reeled in again and got nicely in touch, and there was another pause. The time was 12.30.

The stretch from the Seal to the Verie contained some very large rocks, and consequently a lot of rushing water. There was no proper path on the shore, only rough tussocks of grass and big boulders. But the

Seal was generally a safe place for playing and landing fish, and once we arrived there the Old Man, the ghillie and I heaved a sigh of relief when we saw that salmon, rod and line were all still in touch and as they should be. Here, we thought, will be a fitting end to this already long-drawn fight, and we should be nicely timed and placed for lunch in the bungalow above. The Old Man – still giving the fish all the strain he dared – was sweating quietly and murmuring something about a whisky and soda, as he looked round with longing at the house so near and yet so far. This was an understandable request, and I hurried away, mixed a strong full tumbler and ran back to the pool, hoping I had missed nothing.

Everything was the same, but the ghillie was wading in the edge of the river, trying to see the fish in the dark depths of the water, holding his gaff forward as if it were a beckoning magic wand. We all gazed down, but saw only the line still taut, still cutting slowly and deliberately through the pool. The Old Man gulped his drink quickly, and said his back and arms were getting stiff. It was hardly surprising. The spectators had dwindled a bit, but those remaining were now determined to follow to the end. Some of them had sandwiches, which they offered to the Old Man. He munched them hungrily.

I do not know exactly how long we stayed at the Seal Pool, long enough anyway for me to go to the house again to replenish the tumbler, and cut some bread and cheese into rough sandwiches. The salmon showed no sign of tiring and never once let himself be drawn into view. Then, when the Old Man was making a special effort to coax him up near the surface, he made another wild charge which took him suddenly out of the far side of the Seal and away into the boiling cauldron below. This time the backing really did spin off the reel, and the Old Man, followed by his cavalcade of admirers, was sorely tried over the rough going. It was a nightmare run, because once the fish left the Seal Pool there was no stopping before the upper waters of the Verie, which at this moment seemed miles away. One stumble, one false step, and the gut would have snapped like cotton.

But somehow we all arrived there, still in touch, still intact, mainly owing to the skill and determination of the Old Man, who was by now nearly staggering with weariness. There were more sighs of relief. The Verie really was safe; no big fish ever went further than the small pool at the far end, whence he could nearly always be drawn up, coaxed or forced back into the dark oily safety. Up and down the pool the fight continued, and still no one had seen the fish. The Old Man was more than ever convinced that he must be foul-hooked in the back or belly, and it certainly looked like it; an ordinary salmon, however large, would never have fought so long or so far without his opponent seeing him at some time, even if it were only a glimpse. There was still not the slightest sign of weakness, and several times the fish made a determined effort to run out, refusing always to be drawn upwards, gradually edging down to the shallow part of the tail of the pool. We all told one another that he could not possibly go out, it was so very rare. We were also certain that if the Verie had to be abandoned, then the fight must be lost in the falls between here and the Bothy Pool, a long way below.

With another rush he went out, and so determined was the Old Man's last effort to stop him that he forced the fish into the side of the river below the Verie, where there was a small trout pool under the bank, only a few yards long. The ghillie made a cautious move forward, and I was just behind him. Here, surely, where it was fairly shallow, there might be a last chance to save a situation now looking desperate.

And then the ghillie and I saw something we shall never forget, something you see only in dreams, something that always remains a dream because it could not be real. The salmon, the monster salmon, lay in this little pool for a moment – a colossal greenbacked submarine, bigger than any salmon any angler had ever seen. And the hook was in the side of his mouth, just as it should be. He was well below the surface of the water, swaying gently, and as the ghillie slowly moved the gaff over his back, he gave a lazy supercilious roll, mocked us with a pale silver belly and was gone.

This was more than serious, and there was a general groan of despair. The rapids here were scattered across a shallow river, rapids that ran in narrow fierce streams between immense rounded boulders. There was no quiet water anywhere between the banks until the Bothy Pool was reached. Worse still, round the base of the small precipice on the curve, the only path was a narrow platform built on the steep rock itself. The salmon raced down these rapids, and the Old Man had to run again, rod held ever higher. Any lesser angler would certainly have lost his fish at this stage; indeed, he would have lost it long before; but the Old Man knew every stone and boulder, knew the mysterious underwater paths of salmon, and how to avoid the line billowing or catching on snags. In a way that looked like magic, the rapids were navigated at a murderous pace, and then the demon fish lay sulking in the depths of the Bothy.

Surely this desperate business must soon come to an end; surely either the fish must be landed, the hook pull out of his mouth, or the gut snap with all the punishment it was taking. The time was 1.30, the struggle had gone on now for three hours or more, and it was hard to believe that the salmon did not feel by this time some of the weariness that was showing in the Old Man, who was clearly haggard and suffering physically.

We all knew, however, that now the Bothy had been reached, there was a fair stretch of water below, water containing several small but easy pools where many a fish had been landed. We knew, and the Old Man knew best of all, that there was a good chance now, even if the demon fish broke away again. If only the tackle would hold a little longer, if only the gut did not break! He could go as far as the Stone Pool, if he were still capable of charging downstream, and somewhere between here and that pool we should have him. And then there was the Stone Pool itself, below which no salmon ever went.

Well, he was still capable and set off downstream again, not delaying long in the nice easy pools, not giving anyone much breathing space until he reached the Stone Pool. It was there, white as chalk, shaking all over and streaming with sweat, that the Old Man sat on a rock, still with his rod upright. The few spectators were still with us, fascinated as though hypnotised. I looked carefully at the Old Man, just sitting on the rock, in a trance of near-fainting, and then I did something I had so far hesitated to do – I offered to take the rod and send the ghillie back to the house for more refreshment. Although still game and unwilling to give in, the Old Man had to agree, provided I just kept a strain on the line and no more. The fish was now uncannily quiet. I held the rod as directed, and nothing stirred. I might have been anchored to a rock. The whisky duly arrived and was eagerly swallowed.

The Old Man's face showed grim determination after his refreshment; he got up from the rock rather stiffly and took the rod again. He walked above and pulled, and then pulled from below. Nothing happened.

He asked me if I had felt any slight movement during my vigil, and I assured him there had been none. Had the fish managed to anchor the hook under a snag, and quietly gone away laughing? Such things had happened before. But whether he was still on the end of the line, sulking, or had actually escaped, there was no doubt that this business had to be finished one way or the other in the Stone Pool, the last possible chance before the river ran away in a thundering race below the overhanging trees.

Acting on instructions, I waded and jumped out on the flat rocks that lay at the head of the pool, and threw stones into the water where the taut line disappeared. To everyone's astonishment the fish began to move again. He was even stronger after the long rest, and bolted straight for the tail of the pool, where he paused on the absolute brink, while the Old Man was straining back at him all he could. It simply had to end here; there was no alternative, and the Old Man muttered that it would be better to snap the gut here and now than let the fish out of his last pool.

But he did have to let it go, and once more stumbled and ran among the boulders where the Cruachan Burn empties itself into the Awe. The reel was screaming, the fish already down opposite the trees, the only path on the grassy bank behind. I realised that this was now a matter for teamwork; it did not matter who rushed in now, for this was the end. I plunged downwards, half slipping in the water, underneath the first branches. The Old Man handed me the rod, knowing he could go no farther, and a youth who had been with us all the time, his battered hat decorated with salmon flies, scrambled a few yards below me. The footing could hardly be worse, the pebbly bank sloped straight and steep into the deep scudding water. I reeled in, felt the fish still there, and struggled two yards downwards, hanging on to the

THE ONE THAT GOT AWAY

branches with one hand, the other grasping rod-butt and line together. I managed to hand over to the youth, who also reeled in, trying desperately to hold the salmon from slipping away from us. The Old Man and the others were on the grass path behind the trees, peering through and shouting encouragement.

I struggled down again below the youth, who then repeated my own manoeuvre, and handed the rod back to me. We were more or less hanging in the branches like monkeys. Wonder of wonders, the fish was still firmly at the end of the line. Meanwhile the youth was having a fearful time working himself under thicker, lower branches. Once the shingle on the bank gave way under his feet, spattering into the water; he saved himself only by hanging on to a stout branch. I followed down as well as I could, but by now the rodpoint was forced downwards by the trees, the backing had started to run off the reel, and the fish was a long way off, out in the middle of the rapids.

I shouted to my partner to try to get him back a bit, to reel in as much as he dared, which he did as soon as he took the rod again. At this stage its tip was occasionally hitting the tops of the waves, and there was no hope of keeping it upright. I dropped a bit farther down; all the time the going was more difficult, and we were soaked to the waist. But once more, after a back-breaking effort, the rod was again in my hands, the backing now trailing loosely many yards down the river. I braced hard against a branch that was doing its best to throw me headlong into the water, and reeled desperately. The backing obediently returned, the line, then the gut, and finally the fly.

The monster salmon had gone, the greenbacked submarine would find peace again in the deep pools far below, or even the sea itself. The time was after 2.30 and our estimate of the weight of the fish was between 60 and 70 lbs.

PIE FOR DINNER

Here is another of Billie Flynn's stories. It is concerned with gastromonic, not piscatorial, distress, but I have put it in here in order to cheer you up after the last two tales of tragedy.

W HEN Billie Flynn was fourteen and little more than an errand boy he was the unwitting participant in an incident which caused the Duke of Devonshire and his guests some merriment and the cook at Careysville great anxiety. One evening, Mr Willie Jameson, fishing the Sand Hole and in a state of irritation having just lost a couple of fish, was handed a telegram to the effect that two gentlemen from Lismore Castle would be coming to dinner that evening. Noting Billie walking along the bank opposite he called out, as Billie understood the message, "Tell Cook pie for dinner instead of tea". Billie ran up to the house and told the cook, "Mr Jameson sent me up to tell you pie for dinner instead of tea". Quoting Billie's own words, "Cook got excited and cried, 'We never have tea for dinner. He's mad, he's mad! Will you go down and ask him for what kind of pie does he want?'." Billie, insisting that the cook should accompany him, returned to the river and shouted across to Mr Jameson, "The cook is here, sir. She wants to know what kind of pie do you want for dinner." "God damn her," retorted Mr Jameson, "tell her a magpie!" Cook cried out again, "He's mad. I never heard of a magpie and can't find one and don't know how to cook it!" Billie's conclusion of the story went, "Just at half past seven a big car pulled up at the door and out of it comes the Duke of Devonshire and Sir Claude

Anson. No dinner for them! Mr Jameson rushed to the kitchen: "Why haven't you dinner for these people?" "Why didn't you tell me, sir?" "I sent Billie up to tell you five for dinner instead of three." "Billie told me, sir, pie for dinner instead of tea and you told me to cook a magpie!" Billie, recounting this story, added that they had plenty to eat after all and "laughed until marnin'". He would tell it whenever an opportunity arose. According to him, it was a great favourite of the old Duke who entertained King George V with it when they were shooting together in Scotland.

4

INDEPENDENCE DAY AT MALANGSFOSS

On the morning of 2 July, 1964, I was sitting in a boat in the largest salmon pool in Europe. This was Malangsfoss on the Maals River in Northern Norway. At latitude 69°, it lies half-way between Narvik and Tromsö.

C HARLES Ritz has described Malangsfoss as a salmon aquarium, and indeed it is. The great Maals River, fed by glaciers, tumbles down a mighty waterfall (foss) some half a mile in length and a hundred yards wide. No fish of any species could ascend that *foss* in high water. The artificial salmon ladder was understood to be largely neglected by the most fickle of all sporting fish. The pool, if you can call fourteen acres of turbulence a pool, was fished by two boats with one angler in each, using spoon baits with heavy leads. The boatmen were all members of the Fosshaug family, owners of the pool, and one fished seated in the stern. It would have been impossible to recover even a powerful swimmer had he fallen overboard.

I was one of a party of fishing journalists from France, West Germany, Switzerland, Great Britain and the United States. One of the Americans was Martin Kane, boxing correspondent of *Sports Illustrated* of New York, who had been sent along because the angling correspondent had broken his leg. The other was called Tony Triolo.

I was lucky enough to catch a fish that morning and it was a great moment for me to announce at lunch that I had killed my first Norwegian salmon. My Norwegian hosts and fishing partners were equally delighted and many toasts were proposed and drunk.

The next day, 3 July, proved a great day for the United Nations, all except America killing a fish, despite a rising river. Switzerland got two, each of 23 lbs, and lost two; Germany got two of 17 lbs and 13 lbs, France one of 18 lbs, Norway a grilse of 3 lbs and England two of 20 and 14 lbs. By evening the river had risen appreciably and we decided to abandon the operation at about 9 pm, our day's catch being eight salmon.

On Saturday, 4 July, the stars and stripes was hoisted from the flag-pole and we all hoped that this would be a good omen for Kane and Triolo. In fact there was little fishing that day because the river had risen at least two feet and the whole pool was a raging torrent. However, the ghillies decided that by having two men to row, it would be possible to fish a limited area. At breakfast someone had said what excellent action photographs one could get of the pool from a helicopter. The tour manager was able to arrange this and so it happened that the helicopter was hovering overhead with our cameramen aboard when the boxing expert's lure was seized by a particularly violent fish. But Martin would allow his vigorous opponent no leeway at all and kept a tight grip on the reel. Nearer and nearer to the horizontal came the rod until the fish was pulling directly on the reel. There was an audible twang as the line parted and the observers overhead had to be content with pictures of this short and sorry skirmish.

────────── 5 ──────────

LOSS OF A LEVIATHAN

Mr Kane was not the only one to lose a fish on that trip, as the following sad story, which I wrote for **Salmon and Trout Magazine** *explains.*

W E LEFT Stavanger by special launch at 7 am on Tuesday, 7 July for the Sand River in the Suldal Valley, which lies due north across several fjords. We were to fish the lower beat of the Sand River by courtesy of the owner, Mr Bergerson, who had also placed his splendid fishing lodge at our disposal. For the purpose of accommodating eleven anglers, the party was split into three groups and each group would fish from a boat in periods of one and a half hours.

Forming No 3 group with Mr Myhre and Mr Ring, I had a three-hour wait before my turn to fish came round and I used this time to examine the fishing records and a 63-pounder on the wall of the living room and in making a reconnaissance of the beat. There had been no netting in the Sand, by agreement between the owners, for three years and the river was starting to benefit. The records showed that in July the salmon averaged 20 lbs or more and that they were being caught mostly on prawn with a lesser number on spoon and yellow belly (plug).

Now, although it was raining and continued to rain all day, the water was low and very clear and I had good hopes of using my fly-rod. At the top of the beat there is a vast waterfall which, in early July, is not penetrated by the fish. Below it the river flows through a gorge for about half a mile into the fjord. On the lodge side there are a number of platforms and places from which the bank fishermen can cast and the whole of the stretch holds fish, as we were to discover. The prawn is not allowed below the Foss pool.

At about 12.30 pm No 2 group took over from No 1, whose Norwegian members had had a fair spell of sport with fish of 21 lbs (on prawn from the Foss pool) and of 15 lbs (on spoon from the middle stretch). Our Norwegian photographer, Mr Knudsen, had hooked a large fish on prawn below the waterfall and had fought it down to the landing stage by the lodge when it came unstuck.

Of No 2 group, (France, West Germany, Switzerland and USA) it was Michelot of France who distinguished himself. He hooked a large fish from the platform below the waterfall on a spoon and had to be rowed downstream in pursuit of it. The fish had in fact been foul-hooked in the belly and was uncontrollable. However, Gallic resolution and fine boatmanship prevailed and this fish (26 lbs) was duly brought to the net in a lower pool after a long and exhausting struggle. It was now the turn of No 3 group and I was allotted a boat in the bottom pool where the river enters the fjord. This is mainly a smooth, even-flowing pool with no rapids or visible horrors. Fish were showing at regular intervals and the omens for the fly seemed favourable, although my ghillie thought that the water at about 42 degrees Farenheit was too cold. He was right and my 2/0 Silver Grey was not accepted. Nor was the spoon with which I covered the water after the fly. After half my allotted time had expired the ghillie announced that he was going ashore. I understood it to be his luncheon recess but it was not mine. However, the tour manager was good enough to deputise at the oars and we finished our period without incident.

Further up, Mr Ring had meanwhile hooked a fish on prawn and lost it but came in with a 4 lb seatrout, also on prawn.

During the afternoon my Norwegian hosts invited me to the Atlantic Hotel beat some three miles up river where a fine fishing lodge overlooks two great pools. This is essentially fly water which is at its best in August and which, for between £7 and £8 a day all in, can be fished by arrangement with the Atlantic Hotel.

On our return to Sand we found that France had killed another salmon (22 lbs) also on the spoon. At 7 pm it was group 3's turn again and I was invited to try the Foss pool, a great expanse of white and green foaming torrent at the top, yielding to fast deep water midway and at the tail, where the stream converges between great rocks to a width of some 20 yards.

From the boat I cast a heavily weighted spoon up, down and across the torrent for a while and then gave up my place to Mr Myhre. Once more on land I was strongly advised by Mr Ring to try a prawn on one of the lodge rods. This was an immensely powerful fibreglass pole fitted with a 4½ in. Silex reel carrying some 200 yards of 40 lb b.s. nylon. In view of what followed I was glad that I exchanged my less powerful equipment for the official gear. I have not used a prawn before and got it repeatedly stuck in the bottom from where it was promptly and expertly retrieved by our team of attendant ghillies.

At half past eight when, by common consent, we were about to bring the proceedings to an end my prawn was most savagely taken by something uncommonly heavy which, after trying to haul me into the pool from my perch on top of the rocks, swam relentlessly upstream into the base of the waterfall. It then came back to the taking point and repeated the performance. Evidently I was into one of the Sand monsters and the head ghillie seemed to think so too for, after about ten minutes of impotent hauling, during which no line was recovered, I was directed into the boat and propelled by two pairs of oars across to the other side, where the waters were more placid. Once again, I found myself attached to a heavy fish directly downstream of the boat. After a while the fish ceased to move and we concluded that he was underneath or behind one of the shelving rocks which abound in that part of the pool. The boat was lowered to where the line entered the water and the ghillie secured the line by hand. The fish had got rid of the prawn and had left it attached to the rock from where we recovered it later.

LADY PERCY

Lady Percy had no such problem. When a 15 lb salmon hurled itself uninvited into her lap, she was sufficiently quick witted to clasp it to her bosom. This story is told by her sister, Lady Evelyn Cotterell, in her book *Salmon Fishing on the Spey*.

A POACHER'S DILEMMA

*This tragic little bit of history manqué comes from a book called **I Have Been Fishing**, by John Rennie, who was a champion caster with trout and salmon rods and the winner of many events. In the brief periods between visits to famous streams and rivers in Norway, Iceland, Ireland, Scotland, England and Wales he practised as an engineer and artist, as befitted the grandson of the man who built Old Waterloo Bridge.*

CALDERWOOD told me the story of the great salmon which was caught by a poacher on the River Earn in Scotland some years before this (1934). The legend of this fish, which was reputed to have weighed 102 pounds, is roughly as follows: It was caught by a poacher – how it was caught is not related, but we can assume that it was caught by unfair means. It was so large that the man was afraid to sell it as a whole, so cut it up in pieces. But, before cutting it up, he took it to a neighbouring farmhouse and had it weighed there; it scaled 102 pounds. Calderwood went to the farmhouse as soon as he heard the report and testified that the scales were correct, and was satisfied in his own mind that the recorded weight was correct. I must say I would have like to have met that man. Little did he know that he was making history. Willingly would any of us have paid the fine which might have been inflicted. It was a tragedy which can never be repaired.

CHAPTER THREE
ENDURANCE

ENDURANCE

Ever since books on fishing were first published – and one goes back to AD 169 for the first treatise *The Haleutica of Oppian*, a hexameter poem in five books describing tackle and methods and battles with large fish – no scribe seems to have given a thought to the poor fish in its eternal struggle for survival. No one, that is, who comes to mind except Miss Beamish *(The One That Got Away)*, Henry Williamson in *Salar the Salmon*, Ernest Hemingway in *The Old Man and The Sea* and a new generation of American anglers like Shirley Woods who, out of compassion for a splendid opponent, release their captives to perpetuate the species.

Blame exorbitant rentals, escalating rates paid by riparian owners and the resultant price. Blame everybody, but do not blame the salmon.

It is not their fault that they should have become victims of human avarice on the high seas where they feed and in estuarial waters, many to be netted, on their ascent of rivers where they originated as ova.

This chapter is concerned with endurance – endurance certainly of the fishermen (mostly ladies) but also of the salmon, with no help from mechanical aids and only its own strength, determination and primeval instinct for its salvation.

C.M. WELLS
THE MASTER

*Cyril Mowbray Wells died in August, 1963, in his ninety-third year, and in his long life achieved distinction as both a scholar and a sportsman such as few could hope to rival. The list of his attainments is so long and so varied that the briefest summary must here suffice. Born in 1871, he was educated at Dulwich, where he became senior scholar and captain of the school; he won an open classical scholarship to Trinity College, Cambridge, and graduated with a first in the Classical Tripos, having also gained a blue for cricket and rugby football. In 1893 he became a master at Eton where for many years he taught classics to the sixth form. He was a housemaster from 1905 to 1926. He played half-back for England six times between 1892 and 1897 and also regularly for the Harlequins. He played cricket for Surrey in 1892 and 1893 and for Middlesex from 1894 to 1909 and had the distinction of twice bowling out W.G. Grace. The following account of his angling achievements is taken from the obituary which appeared in the **Salmon and Trout Magazine.***

WELLS' attitude to fly fishing, which he took up at 45, when a damaged knee brought games to an end, was strictly in accordance with his approach towards all he attempted. Nothing short of mastery satisfied him. Method and equipment had to be just right and this requirement, allied to splendid casting with fly and bait, brought him success with trout and salmon which can scarcely ever have been equalled and will never be surpassed.

Although a visitor to the Usk, Brora and Irish Blackwater, and also to Ballynahinch in the time of his friends there, Ranji and C.B. Fry, it is his 25-year tenancy of the Bolstad river in Norway and long membership of the Houghton Club at Stockbridge which figure so prominently in the records he has left.

The Bolstad is a short, deep, fast-running river which flows for about three miles from Osen Lake to a fjord north-west of Bergen. Wells fished it in June-July and sometimes in August from 1920 to 1939 and from 1946 to 1950. In a period of 207 weeks, fishing two rods, he and his guests killed 1,496 salmon weighting 40,896 lbs, at an average weight of 27.3 lbs. Wells' personal record is of such interest, in that he killed every weight from 20 to 58 lbs, missing only 55 lbs, that it is set out below. It will be seen that fish of less than 20 lbs were only deemed worthy of collective mention and that 12 of the bag exceeded 50 lbs. The absence from the list of any fish of 60 lbs and over is due to the fact that they were caught, not by Wells, but by his guests, to whom he always gave the most promising places. One of them, the late Major W.H.S. Alston, killed salmon of 60, 61 and 63 lbs. Wells' bag of 848 was made up as follows:–

Bolstad River

Weight of Fish	Number	Weight of Fish	Number
under 20	171	40	14
20	42	41	11
21	27	42	9
22	25	43	10
23	25	44	10
24	38	45	3
25	42	46	6
26	51	47	2
27	34	48	2
28	49	49	1
29	28		
	532		68

Weight of Fish	Number	Weight of Fish	Number
30	51	50	4
31	32	51	1
32	41	52	2
33	22	53	1
34	29	54	1
35	14	55	—
36	11	56	1
37	12	57	1
38	17	58	1
39	7		
	236		12

In his 80th year he killed his 80th salmon of 40 lbs or over.

Rather more than half of Wells' salmon were killed on prawn, just over a third on fly and the remainder by spinning with spoon, spook and sprat. All but a few were hooked and played from a boat kept on each pool, but the fisherman always came ashore for the gaffing. It was quite usual for a large fish to be hooked at the top of the beat and be landed a mile or two below, but at least one of the "great fish", of which more anon, ran right down into the fjord.

Wells' salmon equipment was simple but powerful. "I only use the strongest," he once remarked to the writer. He used the same rod for both fly and bait fishing, a 13 ft Hardy split-cane with two tops, the shorter and stiffer for bait, and longer for fly. This rod, after several breakages, was gradually reduced to about 12 ft. His flies, Thunder and Lightning, Mar Lodge, Dusty Miller etc, were lightly dressed and tied on double-hooks, preferably with gut eyes. In his view large single hooks were unsuitable for the Bolstad fish whose weight and power tended to enlarge the hold on a dangerous width. The size of flies, mainly 1½ to 4/0, strikes one as being curiously small for such a deep and turbulent river. The reel contained 30 yds of casting line and 200 yds of backing. His casts were specially made for him of heavy twisted gut, tapering from about 30 to 20 lbs b/s. Wells would use only the double "Turle" Knot for attaching the fly.

When bait fishing, what was known then as the "bullet" trace was used. This was made up of twisted gut with a b/s of 20 to 30 lbs. The casting line was secured to the top swivel. A few inches below a second swivel was inserted and to this was attached the "bullet", a round ball of lead with a hole through it. The secret of this device lay in the use of soft copper wire for securing the "bullet" to the swivel and the nature of the attachment was such that, when the "bullet" became snagged, a strong jerk would straighten the wire causing it to drop off and allow the rest of the tackle to be recovered.

Wells fished from the stern of the boat (on the Bolstad the boat always proceeded downstream stern first) and covered every foot of water, whether with fly or bait. He attributed much of his success to the skill and knowledge of his ghillie, Mathias, in whose house Wells and his guests always lodged. The nature of the river and size of the fish required boatmanship of the highest order, for the passage downstream in pursuit of a large salmon was fraught with danger from rocks and rapids.

Wells was so humble and reticent about his achievements that he could seldom be coaxed into speaking of them. It was the writer's good fortune, however, to find him twice disposed to talk about his beloved Bolstad. Sharing a tray of tea with him one evening in the Flyfishers' Club I asked him how he had got on in Norway that season. Had others been present, it was doubtful whether much information would have been imparted. Even so, the conversation opened on an unpromising note. "Oh very poor!" he murmured from behind the *Times* City page. I assumed that this signified the end of the matter but, putting the paper aside, he went on, "Sowerby (Mr Murray Sowerby) did quite well." "Oh really, what did he get?" "His first fish weighed 65 lbs and his second 52!" Next time we met in the Club he was in a more expansive mood and spoke at length about his adventures with three 'great fish'. Wells' assessment of a 'great' salmon was one that in his estimation exceeded 70 lbs. He thought any of the three might have been in the 80-90 lbs category. One of these monsters was hooked on a spoon in the tail end of Osen lake. It was followed unseen right down into the fjord, three miles below, Wells playing it from the stern of the boat which, as always, descended stern first, a risky passage on account of the rapids and rocks which had to be negociated. The first glimpse of the fish that Wells and Mathias had was when it was at last brought to the surface exhausted and ready for the gaff. Alas, its great weight and the length of the encounter had jointly served to widen the hold in its mouth and, as it rolled over, the hooks pulled out.

The other two 'great fish' were also lost near the moment of gaffing when their thrashing tails caught the trace and pulled the hooks out. Mr E.F.J. Baugh, Wells' nephew, to whom I am greatly indebted for much information, recalls that his uncle and he spent a long time in pursuit of a fish in the 80 lb class which, lying underneath a bridge, refused every lure they could contrive. Another burst through the fjord nets, placed near the mouth of the river, submerging one of the oil-drum floats in the process.

Date	Water Ft.	In.	Name.	Beat.	Westminster.	Laycock.	Fish. Corbet.	Hamilton.	No.	Weight.
July 20th		1"	Sandia & Vina.		13 / 24.24.20.17. 24.16.21.17.	21.		26. / 25.22.40.22.	15	352 lb
21st		0"	„ „		24. / 21.21.29.29. 23. 11.	17. 22.		23. 20. 26. 25.12.14.25.19.	17	377 lbs
22nd		—2"	Sandia. Vina & Jra.		nil.	21.18.20.7.	nil.	11.21.	6.	98 lb.

6 8

Summary.

Duke of Westminster.	173	salmon.	3970 lbs.
General. Sir J. Laycock.	154	„ „	3402 lbs.
Major. B. Corbet.	107	„ „	2505 lbs.
Col. D. Hamilton	208	„ „	4939 lbs.
Officers from Yacht "Cutty Sark" & Servants	42		904 lbs.
Total	**684**	**salmon weighing**	**15.720 lbs**

July 7th	1'	5"	Upper Soutyo.	Details of Westminster's big night at Soutyo.

24.45. 22.30.23.20 20.25.
19.31.24.34.17.19 .19 26
24.27. 28 18.24 30.29 20
19.19. 22 20.42 15.24 19
23.

33   **800 lbs**

▲ Extract from the Holkham records, showing massive catches on the River Alta

◄ Viscount Coke on the Alta July 1926 with a few of the day's catch and his ghillie

By courtesy of Viscount Coke D.L.
Copyright Coke Estates Ltd.
Photograph by Jim Lightfoot
from the original

▲ Malangsfoss
July 1964

◄ Jack Chance
at Malangsfoss

Eric Myhre and an ▶
18 lb. fish caught at
Malangsfoss
July 1964

◀ C.M. Wells with two large Bolstad fish

▼ C.M. Wells, over ninety years old, the River Test

Glencalvie Lodge ▲
May 1912, Ghillie
Duncan Macrac
weighs the catch
under the scrutiny
of author's Mother
and Uncle

A 55 lb. fish caught ▶
near Stavanger

▲ Fly Fishing on the
Sand River near
Stavanger

◀ A 58½ lb. fish
caught on the Eira River
Norway 1931

A 30 lb. fish ▶
from the Sand
River

▲ The author at Malangsfoss, Arctic Circle, with Konrad Fosshaug.

SALMO THE CLIMBER

Top of the high altitude class must come a salmon discovered thriving in a small burn on the Cairngorms at over 3,000 feet, a phenomenon observed by two stalkers at Rothiemurchus in the autumn of 1981.

This enterprising fish must have had a most compelling tryst with the lady of his choice at such a height.

If we men, to preserve the human species, were required to travel thousands of miles forwards and backwards from the river of origin to feeding grounds in arctic waters, evading predators, netsmen, poachers and fishermen, jumping up rapids and waterfalls in icy waters, it is doubtful whether even the most ardent lovers would have lasted the course. Inevitably homo sapiens (a misnomer if ever there was one) would by now have become extinct. Endurance is the name of this game.

At a much lower level and sixty years earlier a salmon of 42 lbs played a member of the Flyfishers Club for thirteen hours on the Awe. This fish took a small 'Thunder and Lightning' at 11.50 am on 15 June 1914 – two months before the Battle of Mons. It surrendered at 12.45 am on the 16th and was subsequently preserved in its glass case with gut cast and fly at the Flyfishers' Club. Its captor has not been accorded the same distinction.

PLAYING THE OLD DUKE

Here, by way of a little light relief after the strenuous career of C.M. Wells and the exhausting journey of the mountaineering salmon, is another of Billie Flynn's yarns, in which he tells of the fine spirit of endurance shown by the 9th Duke of Devonshire.

THE old Duke of Devonshire, grandfather of the present owner of Careysville, was, so Billie reported, a beautiful fly fisher but not so good with the bait. He loved to play a fish and didn't care who had hooked it so long as he could take over the rod and finish it off. If a fish was killed which he had not either hooked or played it was not, according to Billie, entered in the game book. All the ghillies were aware of the Duke's amiable eccentricity but it was Billie who, on one occasion, unavoidably contravened his employer's wishes.

It was a wild February afternoon with snow on the ground and high winds. The Duke was asleep in a chair in front of a fire in the hut. Billie was fishing with bait a short distance away. A large salmon was hooked and Billie called out at the top of his voice to alert the Duke so that he could take over the rod and play the fish. When his cries failed to awaken the Duke, Billie found himself in a dilemma. What was he to do? To lose such a fine salmon was unthinkable. So he played it and gaffed it. Having killed the fish he left it still attached to the line by the water's edge where a steep bank screened it and his subsequent activities from the hut some twenty to thirty yards away. He rushed into the hut and awoke the Duke. "Your Honour, there is a big fish on the end of the line. Don't come out, you can do the job from here!" The Duke's chair was then pushed out on to the verandah and the rod thrust into eager hands. Billie then raced back to the spot below the bank, grasped the line and pulled it out as fast as he could. He then waited awhile for the Duke to recover line and then pulled out some more. After some twenty minutes of alternatively taking in line and letting it out, Billie thrust the gaff once again into the dead salmon and brought it to the hut where he showed it to the exhausted angler, still seated in his chair on the verandah.

"My God, what a mad fish!" the Duke is alleged to have observed. "Just look at my fingers!" His fingers were bleeding from cuts imparted by the line in its relentless passage from rod to river. "The wildest fish I ever hooked", continued the Duke. "I've fished in Canada and all over the globe but that fish I will never forget. At one time I was on the point of running down to you for help but thank God I managed him myself. No one will ever catch a fish again from the verandah!" Billie praised the Duke for his handling of this mad fish which weighed 27 lbs and was covered with sea-lice. In telling the story he would add "But the Duke never knew it was meself he was stuck into!"

PLAYING THE OLD DUKE

THE MARKETING OF
LADY LIVERPOOL'S FISH

*This short anecdote shows that the battle is not
necessarily over when the adversary has been gaffed,
beached, tailed or otherwise overcome. There is still
scope for the economically minded to display
amazing resources of tenacity and endurance.*

CONSTANCE, Lady Liverpool, who, sadly, died in
1976, once killed a fish of 34 lbs on the Helmsdale. At the time it was believed to be the record for
the river, not notable for salmon of over 20 lbs. I
cannot personally testify to the accuracy of the
epilogue which follows. It may be legendary.

Lady Liverpool's hostess at that time, a sporting
lady with a keen appreciation of the value of such a
large fish, set off with it by night-train to London. A
taxi took her and the salmon to the Guards' Club
where she asked the catering manager whether he
would buy it and at what price.

The figure quoted being unacceptable, the gallant
lady made a round of other clubs, but none would
offer her price.

By this time the fish was starting to show un-
mistakeable signs of deterioration in the warm
weather, a fact which was at once detected by a
fishmonger at Billingsgate Market. However, our
heroine did not readily abandon her project. Back she
went to the Guards' Club where, because of the now
potent aroma, she felt herself able to accept a lower
price than that originally offered. Thus relieved of her
decomposing burden, she returned to Scotland the

THE MARKETING OF
LADY LIVERPOOL'S FISH

same evening, having established a record for the
most costly and most travelled fish from British
waters.

——————5——————

MISS BALLANTINE'S
64-POUNDER

I AM aware that many salmon of over 40 lbs have
been caught by ladies, particularly on the Avon,
Awe and Wye, as well as in Ireland and Norway; but
since these successes have already appeared in
books and articles I have not included them. Likewise
Miss Ballantine's 64-pounder on the Glendelvine
beat of the Tay on a September evening in 1922. She
had, in the morning, already killed fish of 17, 21 and
25 lbs. A dramatic account of her fight with the

monster, which ended long after darkness, has been published in *The Field* and elsewhere. Her father, head ghillie to Sir Alexander Lyle, would not allow his daughter to hand over the rod during the two-hour struggle. Indeed, it would have been impossible for her to have done so, since the management of the boat kept him and the oars at full stretch. Had he not been a man of considerable acumen and power, it is doubtful whether the fish could have been secured.

The circumstances of the final triumph, half a mile downstream, have always fascinated me and may be worthy of repetition. With aching arms Miss B reeled in the fish so close to the boat that they could feel that the line entered the water vertically. Now came Mr B's great moment. He had to make certain of the salmon's depth. Having made up the gut cast himself, he knew that there were five blood-knots in it. By cautious probing with the head of the gaff, he was able to count the knots from top to bottom. When he had counted the fifth he knew the depth and position of the head. And so he was able to gaff it at the first attempt and to haul it over the gunwales.

But the fish, after more than two hours, was by no means exhausted and leaped about in the boat.

"Father thought it was going to jump back into the river and threw himself on top of it. My arms felt paralysed and I was so utterly weary that I could have lain down beside the fish and slept!" It still holds the British record on rod and line and is unlikely ever to be surpassed.

—————————6—————————

MRS JESSIE TYSER

To speak of endurance in the context of this book and not to mention Mrs Jessie Tyser's achievements on the Brora would be like writing a thesis on 20th-

Century golf without mentioning that most illustrious player, Miss Joyce Wethered, now Lady Heathcoat-Amory, and also a flyfisher of distinction.

IT is not so much the size of Mrs Tyser's fish killed at Gordonbush and Balnacoil since 1921 which attracts admiration, but their number. She did indeed land a 29½-pounder, but never equalled in weight the fish of 44,40 and 40 lbs caught by tenants in the lower part of the Brora.

Not once but three times Mrs Tyser achieved "the treble": on 27 September, 1926, with a 7 lb salmon, three grouse and a switch weighing 15 stone; ten years later, on 22 August, 1936, two salmon, a 13-stone stag and three grouse (also two snipe); on 30 September, 1954, a 12 lb salmon, another 15 stone switch and four grouse.

On 18 May, 1962, the water at Balnacoil was perfect, having settled down after a heavy spate which had brought up a large run of clean fish. By breakfast time twenty-one had been killed and by the end of the day the bag totalled fifty-three, a record for the river, and all on the fly. On that particular day some friends of mine were fishing the Dunrobin beat below Brora Loch and never even saw a sign of a salmon. They had all raced upstream to concentrate in a narrow, placid stretch of the river at Balnacoil.

Thrice on the Brora Mrs Tyser accounted for twenty-one in a day and once twenty-two. Before the 1939 war she had killed many large salmon and sea-trout on the Norwegian Stryn, but it is the Bora with which her name will always be associated and esteemed.

CHAPTER FOUR
ELATION

ELATION

1

I have chosen to call this last chapter "Elation" because the stories in it seem to cause merriment among anglers; so it is not surprising that Billie Flynn is again to the fore. It is a sad truth that Billie's stories lose much of their zest when committed to paper, nevertheless I think that they are worth reading and I hope that you will agree.

A SPEYSIDE FUNERAL

*This story is taken from a book called **Sporting Years** published in 1903 and written by Lieutenant-Colonel Andrew Haggard, the brother of Sir Henry Rider Haggard. My son-in-law is a Speyside Grant and I would like to believe that the characters, other than the gravediggers, were related to him. The doctor, evidently not a Grant, to whom the ghillie alludes from time to time with unconcealed venom, had earlier incurred his wrath with a disparaging observation.*

THE ancient ghillie, however, once my persecutor was out of hearing, made some very forcible remarks anent "a daft English body wha kens naething aboot the fesh nor the feshin' ava."

And as we started and continued flogging the water for a long time without the slightest signs of success, his ire against the learned light of the Divorce Court only increased more and more. Nevertheless he made me work all the harder, explaining to me that "if ye want fesh ye maun wet your feet". He persuaded me to wade deeper and deeper into the rapid waters of the Spey until I could scarcely keep my footing on the loose stones at the bottom. It was, however, then that I found out the advantage of having the gran' tackets at the bottom of my boots – both east and west.

At length, after wearily fishing for long, without ever a rise, we reached a certain pool opposite a cemetery across the river. There was a funeral going on when we reached this spot, and my sense of the decorous was disturbed. I did not think it right to be wildly waving a salmon rod in full sight of the mourners, and said so. Andrew Grant did not agree with me. His remarks were caustic. "Whisht, mon, haud yer tongue, dinna fash yersel', yon's the buryin' o' Mistress Grant, the wife o' Hugh Grant, the factor up the Strath, an' himself the grandest fesher in a' Strathspey; it's no' for him ye'll need to stop the feshin', and' the meenister another fesher forbye. Losh! If ye could but joost hook a fesh the noo ye'd be doin' a vera meritorious action, an' mebbe dispel his sad thochts. See the buryin's over, and yon's Hugh Grant himsel', he wi' the beard, an' three ithers, wi' their white hankies in their han's, comin till the watter side forenent us. Man! ye'll have to get a fesh the noo; a funeral's gey lucky for this pool ava."

Sure enough as I waded out into the pool I was able to remark a party of mourners, consisting of two ladies and two gentlemen, leaving the open grave, and coming down to the river's bank to watch me, all attired as they were in their sombre garments. It made me feel nervous, for I feared greatly to bungle in some way before this gallery of spectators, among whom was "the grandest fisher on Speyside!"

There was in the middle of the pool a large rock showing in the low water a little above the surface, and my worthy ghillie told me that "ahint the big stane" was the sure lie of a fish. He insisted that I must reach this spot with the fly, but it seemed just a yard or two farther than I could attain, let me wave and thrash with the big rod never so wildly. But leaning hard against the current, I took just two steps farther out, and the fly fell at length upon the desired spot. Heavens! There was a rise – a splendid rise of a big salmon, a few yards below the boulder. But the fish had not taken the fly.

"Rest him a bittie," cried Grant, "an then try him agen. What time will it be the noo whateffer?"

"Five minutes to four," I replied, as I wheeled in the slack of my line, and went back to the bank side.

"Oh! ay. Then ye'll just rest him the five meenits. Ye ken yon daft liar mon" – I hope he meant lawyer man – "was sayin' that sic a gran' fesher as you wad be for gettin' three fesh atween four an' sax o'clock. Maybe the laugh will no' be on the doctor's side the nicht. Just bide the five meenits an' you'll ha' yon fesh, as sure's saxpence. Lord, there's the meenister," he added hurriedly; "Ay, 'tis Mr Grant himsel' come doun forenent us to watch the feshin'."

With an inward groan, I perceived that it was true enough. The minister had come to join the other spectators on the bank. There only now remained the gravediggers.

I supposed that they were Grants also, and would be there presently too to look at me. Being somewhat nervous – as who would not have been under the circumstances? – I honestly wished that the whole lot could then and there have been buried – temporarily – in one huge mausoleum inscribed in gigantic letters with the name of Grant. But since this was impossible, I pretended not to see the surviving Grant clan, and, at four o'clock precisely, waded out into the river again.

Two minutes later I placed the Wee Professor, as the fly I had on was called, once more on the right spot behind the stone. Instantly there was a big boil on the surface. I struck heavily, and in a second the rod was bent double – the big fish was on, firmly hooked. A fine devil's dance it was that he led me, especially as, struggling backwards, foot by foot, against the heavy current, I sought to regain *terra firma*. Once on dry land I had, from the top of a high bank, more command of the salmon, "a most terrible monster whateffer," as Andrew Grant called him, that repeatedly sprung out of the water like a prancing porpoise.

Meanwhile, all the ministers and mourners on the opposite bank – I mean all the Grants, for they had ceased to mourn – were dancing about in their excitement like cats on hot bricks; and while minister Grant shouted to me not to hold him too hard, but to give him line, the newly made widower Grant yelled to me: "Give him the butt, man – give him the butt."

SPEYSIDE FUNERAL

And, of course, just as I had expected, the two gravedigger Grants now rushed, spade in hand, to the shore to watch the fun also. Oh! how I hoped and prayed that the whole crowd of them might not be witnesses of my final discomfiture. The salmon was a clean-run fish, evidently just from the sea, and as strong as a lion, and I was tired long before he was. Repeatedly he took out most of my line. At length he ceased to make splendid runs and dashing leaps, commencing to roll over and over on the surface of the water. This was awful!

"He's gettin' gey tired the noo," cried Grant; "can ye no' get him to the side? But, man!" he almost screamed in his excitement, "how will I get him oot? I've no' a handle to my gaff!'

He held up to my horrified gaze a rough blacksmith-made gaff hook with a long iron shank, which he should have whipped with cord on to a stick before we

began fishing. But in spite of his anger against the doctor, he had evidently thought our chance of a fish so infinitesimal that he had neglected to do so.

"You must just do your best without a handle," I said gloomily; "hold the shank in your hand, and strike so."

Then giving the salmon the butt more and more, I brought him at length to the very bank side. There the little man was crouching motionless, grasping his hook by the shank, and waiting for his prey. Suddenly a dash on the part of Grant – a horrid jar on the line – a frightful splash of the salmon – and then instead of his being brought to land, the fish was dashing out into the middle of the river once more, apparently as strong as ever. There was a horrified yell from the throats of all the Grants in the graveyard opposite, which struck terror into my heart as though it had been their own war slogan of old. For I thought, with them, that the salmon was off. But no; he was still on secure, as the screech of the reel soon told. What had happened was this. The wretched old gaff was so blunt that, when the ghillie had struck, the point had failed to penetrate the skin, but had scored all up the fish's side.

"Losh he here!" cried the disconsolate Grant, as he looked ruefully at the point of his gaff, "I'll swear that gin ye'll gie me aniter clip at him he'll no' escape a second time."

As I once more began to feel and get command of my salmon, the minister and the factor began also to shout advice to the ghillie, one of them crying: "Tail him, man, tail him"; the other with sundry swear words remarking that he was a – well – something fule not to get the salmon by the gills.

To make a long story short, although the salmon had got canny, and repeatedly dashed away again whenever I pulled him anywhere near the ghillie, his enemy, whom he now knew well by sight, at length the man got another chance. This time he struck right underneath the fish at the softest part of the belly. There was an awful splashing and a struggling, and then little Grant, with both his arms clasped tightly round the great mass of silver, which looked as long as himself, came staggering up the steep bank, to the paean of encouraging cheers from across the water. In these the ladies joined vigorously while waving their black-edged handkerchiefs, the minister, factor, and grave-diggers waving their hats. At that proud moment if I had had a shipload of gold, instead of using it to erect a mausoleum, I would willingly have devoted it to raising a magnificent monument to the Clan Grant.

As for the ghillie, when at length he released his fervent embrace of that salmon, his sole remark was, "That'll be one for the daft doctor whateffer." The fish weighed 27 lbs. Fortunately one of the ghillies from the lodge, Johnny Grant by name, happened to come up just at that moment. Him we sent up with the beautiful salmon to the lodge, with a sarcastic message to the effect that the other two would be ready to follow by six o'clock. And, *mirabile dictu*, they were; one was a 13-pounder and the other exactly 10 lbs in weight.

Shouting friendly farewells to my friends on the opposite bank, I returned to my hotel, where the news of my success had preceded me. That night the laugh was not on the doctor's side at dinner! Indeed, to this day he has never been allowed to forget the three salmon whose funeral obsequies were performed between four and six.

LADY LONDONDERRY'S HERRING

Here is another story of Billie Flynn's and if, in fact, it should be called "The Duchess of Northumberland's Herring" I make due apology to her memory.

IN his latter years Billie would get a bit confused about the identity of the dramatis personae who figured in some of his tales. Thus the following episode was sometimes attributed to the late Duchess of Northumberland and at others to the late Marchioness of Londonderry. He would begin by saying that he was introduced to this distinguished lady, a guest of the Duke, and she had expressed a wish to catch a fish and was asking what sort of fish they kept in the river at Careysville.

"Well, Ma'am, we've salmon an' peal and trout an' pike, an' roach an' eels – an' red herrings," added Billie for good measure. "Which one do you fancy, Ma'am?". When the lady said that she was fond of a nice red herring for her dinner and opted for that particular fish, Billie found himself in a serious dilemma. However, the arrival of the luncheon interval before fishing could begin enabled him to prepare and execute a plan by which the lady's wish could, with luck, be gratified. Asking her to meet him at the fishing hut after lunch, he cycled into Fermoy and bought a few herrings which he stuffed into a pocket and rode back. He then dug up some worms, selected a stout rod and fixed two hooks to the gut cast, one at its end and the other a foot or two above it. In due course the lady arrived at the hut and they moved off along the riverside. Billie chose a stretch of the river where the bank rises high above the water level and it was there that he invited the lady to sit down on the grass at some distance from the bank so that he would be out of her sight. A bunch of worms was threaded on to the lower hook and the herring secured to the upper hook. He then tossed the lot into the river a few yards out, climbed up the bank and handed the rod to the lady. Billie knew that it would not be long before an eel would be attracted to the worms. Allowing a few minutes for them to be assimilated, he invited the lady to raise the rod and strike. The playing of the eel had the effect of imparting movement to the herring on the upper hook so as to simulate a live fish. "See, Ma'am, 'tis a foine herrin' ye are after hookin'. Just reel in the loine an' oi'll get the net under 'em!" Billie then slid down the bank, grasped the line and with a knife severed the gut between the eel and the herring. He then netted the fish and, climbing up the bank again, presented it to the lady. "And now, Ma'am, ye'll be after eatin' a lovely fresh herrin' for yer supper!"

3

RODEO ON THE WYE

*To explain the curious title of this piece would be to give the game away, so I must simply ask you to read on. I wrote it for the **Salmon and Trout Magazine**.*

ONE has heard of fishermen who, after decades of successful encounters, find the playing of a salmon tedious once they have established that it is firmly attached. The rod is then handed to a ghillie and the angler retires to the fishing hut for repose and refreshment.

The account which follows is mainly for the benefit of such people, with the purpose of introducing them to an unconventional method of bait fishing and thereby perhaps of resuscitating a vanished interest in that part of the struggle which follows the strike.

At 8 am on a bitter windy morning in March, having risen early for an hour's spinning before leaving the Herefordshire Wye after breakfast, I was contemplating the forbidding scene, alone and palely loitering.

There the analogy with Keats' Knight-at-Arms ends for, although the sedge had long since withered and no birds were singing, there was no belle dame in sight, only a couple of zealous anglers on the opposite bank, pale warriors perhaps but hardly kings and princes.

I had had the good fortune on the two preceding days to catch fresh fish of 16 to 24 lbs on a brown and gold minnow, the larger in a spot where a cluster of boulders parts the current to create a less boisterous retreat behind it, and where I now decided to make a start.

After a few inaccurate sighting casts which brought no more than assurance that my line was not kinked, the bait properly weighted, and that the water was uncommonly cold, I noticed a disturbance some fifty yards above and about twenty-five yards out from my bank. The lynx-eyed warriors opposite, it seemed to me, observed it too but the lie was on my side of the river and, as I thought, out of range from the other bank.

To reach a good position for the assault on what seemed certain to be a taking fish, I had to penetrate a jungle of dead undergrowth and to pass over some slabs of rock sloping riverwards with a miniature cliff behind, studded with saplings to restrict the cast. A competent bait caster with a fixed spool reel would have found no problem in flicking the minnow to the desired spot, but I am not one of these and my equipment would probably earn the scorn of an expert. However, my bait did land for once where directed at the first attempt and was at once seized, as it came over the lie, with a vicious tug. Immediately the fish made off at top speed across and obliquely down stream – the river is eighty yards wide at this point – and a rapid calculation indicated that a distance of some one hundred and twenty yards separated us, leaving a paltry thirty yards of line on the reel.

I must at all costs keep abreast of this formidable springer, so I retreated from my slab of rock and made my way downstream at such speed as my waders and the obstacles would permit. My modest progress had something in common with the fathers' sack race on a school sports day.

This manoeuvre, so far from reducing the distance between rod and fish, merely served to spur my adversary to greater endeavours. Finding that he could go no further in the direction of his first choice without ascending the opposite bank, this violent fish spurted off downstream at a rate which had my reel screaming in protest. I was now confronted with a fresh problem for a row of pollarded elms separated me and my opponent. Far too deep for wading and quite impossible to pass by the trees on the land side. I came to my senses as the last few yards of line were stripped off to expose an almost naked drum, and scrambled up the muddy bank to a path some twelve feet above water level. With rod extended vertically the line just cleared the elms, but only just.

At half-past eight the engagement showed no signs

of a conclusion and I now thought it possible that this uncooperative salmon must be one of those Wye monsters which, according to the books, have kept their captors fully extended until after nightfall. Time and again, this one had me running at my best rate up and down the bank and along the path with never less than eighty yards of line out and often more.

By nine o'clock my mind was preoccupied with thoughts of search parties, bonfires, whisky flasks pressed by kind hands to quivering lips and all the paraphernalia of a desperate finale. An awareness of increasing fatigue brought home the fact that I would soon be incapable of further physical exertion on a scale demanded by this frenzied creature.

So far and no further, I muttered to myself in the manner of one who has found a shell hole in no-man's land – But this was no shell hole, only a little inlet, with a patch of grass on which to recline. I sat down in this oasis, gripped the reel handles and applied to the rod all the pressure I could muster. How would the fish, still unseen, respond to this display of resolution?

There was a moment of extreme tension when neither participant would yield an inch and then the pressure slackened a trifle but just enough to allow me by pumping – I borrow the term from the shark fishermen – to recover a few feet of precious line.

The fish must have sensed that a new spirit had entered the contest for it allowed itself, albeit with reluctance, to be brought foot by foot across the river to within fifteen or twenty yards of my little bay. It was then that I saw my opponent for the first time, no Wye monster alas, only a fish of moderate size. But why had he fought so powerfully and without respite for an hour and why did he now persist in coming in broadside on?

Hooked in the dorsal fin perhaps – Very well, he's still going to pay for his carelessness, for wasting my time and for reducing me to the last stage of exhaustion. I continued the pumping procedure. When the salmon had been brought to within a few yards I observed with alarm that the nylon trace formed a coil around the midriff and that none of the treble hooks were embedded in either fin or flank – One of them had caught up in the nylon trace to form a noose which encircled the body just behind the dorsal fin.

The salmon's first glimpse of his adversary was not apparently a favourable one for summoning its last resources it made a spirited dash across the river. Oh Lord, I thought,here we go again and my thoughts reverted to the search parties, bonfires and whisky – but my anxiety was unfounded. This sortie was in fact the last. The fish, a hen of 15½ lb., allowed herself to be towed within reach and my telescopic gaff concluded the proceedings.

The sad manner of her end may well have been spread around amongst her friends and relations that day from How Caple to Brockhampton. You can imagine the gossip, "I always said that woman would come to a bad end", or, "Just like the old girl to get herself lassoed". Lassoing a salmon may not be strictly ethical yet I commend the technique to those anglers for whom the playing of one conventionally hooked no longer offers any excitement.

4

HOW TO CATCH
A SALMON WITH A
PUNT POLE

*Back to Billie again; and I can vouch for the truth of
this story since I was one half of the cast of two.*

BILLIE and I once found ourselves in a situation
which taxed even his inventive capacity. I must
explain that a hot lunch was served each day at 1
o'clock in the fishing hut and that one was expected to
be punctual for it. It was 12.30 pm when Billie and I
reached the lower part of the Barriers Pool, having
fished down with the fly without a touch. From the
Barriers to the fishing hut one has either to cross the
river by boat and walk for half-an-hour or go by car a
distance of six or seven miles round by Fermoy. We
had a car with us on this occasion and would therefore
have to leave in it no later than 12.40 pm.

The river was very high for mid-summer and Billie
could not bear to leave this fine pool empty-handed.
"Just try a cast or two with the bait," he urged. I put a
small minnow across the stream below the lower
Barrier (a large submerged rock in the middle) and
worked my way downwards. A fish seized the bait
after the second or third cast but came off almost at
once. "The Divil an' all," observed Billie, "just one
more for luck!" I cast again and as the minnow came
round in the deep water below the rock it was seized
by a strong fish which had me and my light spinning
rod at a disadvantage. After a surge upstream, the
fish, playing very deeply, turned back to the spot
where it had taken the bait. There it stayed, rooted to

the bottom and nothing we could do could shift it. After some attempts to exert pressure from above it, opposite it and below it and at letting out line to allow the current to apply a pull from downstream, I glanced at my watch. It was 12.50 and I told Billie that we had better cut the line and go home for lunch. This proposal fell on deaf ears.

"We'll try the boat," he announced. Billie was not a great performer with a punt pole, at least not in a very strong current, and we were soon swept downstream from our target with the reel screeching and the rod at a dangerous curve. Billie, now showing every symptom of exhaustion, allowed me to exchange the rod for the pole and I was˜ able to bring the boat upstream to the point where the line entered the water. "Tis one of them poacher's hooks at the bottom you're after bein' stuck in," he called out. "Better cut the loine, the fish'll be away long since." As I was pondering on this advice, I called Billie's attention to a flash of silver ten or fifteen yards downstream of the boat, now anchored. "Glory be to God, 'tis the fish! He's still on! We'll have him yet!" Billie then directed me to try and get hold of the line between the fish and the obstacle which held it fast. I was able to do this by probing with the gaff. I then pulled in line slowly and brought the fish upstream towards the stern of the boat. Billie, meanwhile, had been leaning on the punt pole to relieve pressure on the anchor and, as the fish came alongside, contrived to get the pole entangled with the line. Whether this happened by accident or by intent the effect was to jerk the line out of my hand so that the fish was in fact held by line attached to the pole. Billie, now grunting with his exertions and exhorting the deity with some vehemence, swung the pole towards me and brought the fish near enough for me to gaff it and pull it aboard. I took up the rod again to find that the line from it was still firmly held by the obstacle on the bottom. To try and disentangle it would make us even later for lunch, so we cut the line and punted ashore. On the way home Billie explained that the obstacle around which the fish must have wound the line was one of a number of large cast-iron hooks sunk in the river bed many years before to prevent poachers netting that part of the pool. The fish weighed 12 lbs and was borne into the fishing hut by an exultant Billie. Our late arrival for lunch was excused when the reason for it had been explained and Billie had supplemented his vivid account with a wealth of detail, much of it improvised in the telling. Thus, "How I caught a salmon with a punt pole" was added to Billie's store of fishing sagas.

HOW TO CATCH A SALMON
WITH A PUNT POLE

WHAT IS A KELT?

Mr Davies of Teifi needs no introduction from me.
He speaks for himself.

O NE of the members of the Bledisloe Committee,
set up in 1960 to revise the Salmon and Fresh-
water Fisheries Act of 1923-1935, was a Mr Davies,
one of the last of the coracle netsmen on the Teifi
river in North Wales.

In the course of the investigation Mr Davies, who
wore the same suit on all occasions, having no other,
formed a firm and enduring friendship with his
chairman, Viscount Bledisloe, of Lydney Park,
Gloucestershire. Evidence was taken from many
authorities concerned with trout and salmon. Among
them was a delegation of industrial leaders headed by
the Chairman of the Imperial Tobacco Co. and the
Deputy Chairman of I.C.I. It was hoped to acquire
data from these eminent men of commerce which
might affect the welfare of game fish in rivers, streams
and lakes, particularly on matters concerning pollution,
abstraction, etc, where factories drew their water
from rivers and, in return, discharged effluent sometimes bearing destructive chemicals. At the conclusion
of a long session, Mr Davies, hitherto silent, asked
permission to put a question. This was granted.

"My Lord Chairman – I would like to ask these
gentlemen what is a Kelt?"

After a period of whispering into cupped ears with
attendant expressions of ignorance, there was an
ominous silence.

"It is as I thought, my Lord Chairman," announced
the triumphant Mr Davies. "None of these gentlemen

know what is a Kelt! I respectfully suggest that no notice whateffer be taken of their effidence!"

Note:– A Kelt is a salmon of either sex which, after spawning, descends ultimately in an emaciated condition to the sea. But most do not survive the reproduction procedure.

6

SMOKED PIKE

I hope the reader will not think that I am showing undue favouritism if I let Billie have the last word.

I HAD been cross with Billie for his clumsy efforts to use the net in the manner of a bludgeon. He had, it seemed to me, attempted to stun the fish into submission as it lay gasping in a few inches of water. Disenchanted with my display of intolerance, he had deserted me to seek the consolation of my wife on the bank. I resumed my fishing, at once hooked another fish, beached it and then hooked another. While I was playing fish number three or number four, I was distracted by loud peals of feminine laughter. Billie, having abandoned me, was entertaining my wife with the following story.

Much addicted to pike fishing, he had killed a very large specimen the previous winter. In relating the event to Mrs X., a member of the Wills tobacco family and a regular spring visitor to Careysville, he added that he had cut open the monster's stomach.

"And what did you find inside?" asked the lady, no doubt anticipating the customary store of half-digested wildfowl and miscellaneous bones.

"Just a little jack pike of 2 or 3 lbs," replied Billie.

"And what was it doing inside the monster?" persisted Mrs X.

"Smokin' a Wills Goldflake, ma'am," said Billie.

SMOKED PIKE

—1—
ANGLING LITERATURE

—2—
SOME OF THE
GREAT SALMON FISHERS

ANGLING LITERATURE

I feel bound to offer the theory, but theologians will dissent, that the first reference to salmon is to be found in Psalm 68:–

"When the Almighty scattered Kings in it, it was white as snow in Salmon"

Whether King David (not identified in the Old Testament as an angler, although undeniably a poacher in other men's preserves) was referring to the Sea of Galilee or the Jordan is a matter of speculation; certainly not the Dead Sea, whose abnormal saline content has never supported life. Just imagine game-fish in the Sea of Galilee! Poor things, eking out a precarious existence with scattered Kings cluttering up the place. That they were white as snow is no surprise – evidently in the terminal stage of a revolting disease, implanted by decomposing monarchs.

Scriptural research reveals that the Kishon in Galilee was a spate river, susceptible to drought. Bloodthirsty Elijah had all the prophets of Baal slaughtered there (I Kings XVIII) thereby imperilling its purity.

So, by and large, it is doubtful whether the Kishon ever supported fish life. We shall never know how many fine lakes and rivers were defiled by the custom of chucking corpses into them in the name of Jehovah.

The horror reappeared in certain British rivers in the 1880's, notably Dee, Tweed, Eden, Derwent, Kent and further south, but not in the name of religion.

Proclaimed by ichthyologists and piscine under-takers as U.D.N. – Ulcerative Dermal Necrosis (no

– 97 –

connection with the United Nations) – the killer reappeared with devastating effect in County Kerry 1963/64. It has been with us ever since apart from periods of misleading alleviation.

Subsequently, this malignant disease has become more widely known as U.F.O. – Unidentifiable Fish Occultism – or something like that. The definition varies from time to time in accordance with current scientific idiom. 'Salmonella' is the latest. The nomenclature is misleading. Although the bacteria may have generated from unsealed tins of Pacific salmon, so far the casualty rate is mercifully minimal. There is no evidence at all of infection from this source of *salmo salar*. Earlier (Numbers XI.5) "The children of Israel mourn for the fish which they did eat in Egypt freely with cucumbers, melons, leeks, garlic and onions." No luxuries allowed by Moses during Exodus. Undoubtedly the Israelites had never had it so good during their sojourn in Egypt. There is no specific identification with *salmo salar*, of course, but, with all those delectable concomitants, (just what you would expect at Royal Ascot or the Lord Mayor's Banquet) one wonders.

ΊΧΘΥΣ

Don't believe what the pundits love to breathe into your ear, or eye. The first complete treatise on fishing is the **Halieutica** of Oppian (circa AD 169), a hexameter poem in five books. It contains information about tackle and methods. There are descriptions of battles with big fish narrated in a spirit of enthusiasm.

The first reference in literature to fly-fishing is in the fifteenth book of Aelian's **Natural History** (3rd century AD) – how the Macedonians captured a spotted fish in the River Astraeus with a lure made up of coloured wool and feathers, used, one suspects, in the manner now known as dapping.

The Odyssey reveals that fishing with rod and line was understood in early Greece and used as a popular illustration. Herodotus has several references to fish and fishing. Plato's *Laws* mentions the capture of fish. Aristotle deals with fish in his *Natural History*.

Pliny devoted his 9th book of *Natural History* to fishes and wild life. Plautus, Cicero, Catullus, Horace, Juvenal, Pliny and Suetonius all allude to angling here and there.

In AD 320 Ausonius in the *Mosella* deals with fish in the Moselle and methods of capture. In this poem is found the first recognisable description of *salmo salar* and *salmo fario*.

Asphalim (Theocritus, 21st Idyll) relates a dream in which he hooked a large golden fish and describes how he played it. (Anyone with a suburban garden pool could have done as well!)

Martial provides the earliest notice of private fishing rights in his epigram *Ad Piscatorium* which warns poachers against fishing in the Baian Lake, wherever it may be. I am unlikely to trespass.

If the reader is not by now entirely bored by this early stuff, well – I am! But I regard it as my duty to proceed a little further – a few centuries, no more. So stifle your yawns and bear with me.

Earliest Reference In English

Aelfric, Archbishop of Canterbury, AD 995, preferred fishing in the river to fishing in the sea. If that is his only mark on history, I don't think much of Aelfric. I hope the present incumbent will be remembered for more positive achievements.

The British Museum has a manuscript *Comptes*

de Pêcheries de l'Eglise de Troyes (AD 1349-1413). This tract gives a detailed account of fisheries, with weight of fish captured and cost of working. Characteristically French – the cost, I mean.

First Printed Book On Angling

Printed in Antwerp circa 1492 by Matthias Van der Goes (ex. Denison Library): "This book teaches how one may catch birds . . . and fish with the hands, and also otherwise." Twenty-five translated copies were printed privately for Alfred Denison in 1872. But in 1502 a German edition had appeared. I am not all that keen on catching birds or fish by sleight of hand. Leave that to the poachers and conjurors. But this I know – Alfred Denison's collection of books on angling was unrivalled. A separate room at Ossington Hall (demolished after wartime Army occupation) housed the finest private collection of early fishing books.

Some of them found their way after the Sotheby's sale to Princeton University via Otto von Kienbusch, America's leading collector of angling literature and fly-fishing rods of the classic periods. After that sale, perhaps the most important of angling works ever held, he wrote to me:–

"The Ossington sale of fishing books was disappointing. Prices were very high and I was able to secure only seventy lots!"

In 1496 appeared *Treatyse of Fisshinge with an Angle* printed in Westminster by Wynkyn de Worde, part of the second edition of the *Book of St Albans*. This famous work, so often quoted and so readily attributed to the sporting nun, Dame Juliana Berners, has become Holy Writ amongst fishing authors. It would be wise to bear in mind that there is no evidence of authorship. It was more likely a compilation from earlier works on angling, possibly a MS of 15th century writings (Denison Library). The list of twelve trout flies from the *Treatyse* survives in many fishing books into the 18th century.

Are you still awake? I suppose we'd better start to conclude this saga of angling literature up to a time when records, methods and assorted expertise have still to acquire the imprimatur of history.

1590   L. Mascall did little more than edit the *Treatyse*.

1613   *Secrets of Angling* by John Dennys (in verse).

1614   Gervase Markham, *Pastes and Flies for Salmon*.

1651   *The Art of Angling* by Thomas Barker, a book commended by I. Walton.

1652   *The Compleat Angler*. Five editions were printed in Walton's lifetime. The final edition incorporated Charles Cotton's contribution. Walton was not a fly-fisherman. Cotton was, and his memorial tablet was placed by the Flyfishers Club in St James's Church, Piccadilly.

1658   *Northern Memoirs* by Richard Franck, in which he advocated the dressing of many salmon flies.

1662   *The Experienced Angler* by Robert Venables. He was Cromwell's least successful commander, leading several expeditions which ended in disaster. Happily, his reputation was redeemed by this book which was warmly commended by Walton.

Other 17th Century Fishing Books

The Gentleman's Recreation by N. Cox.
The Angler's Delight by Gilbert.
The Complete Troller by R. Nobbes.
The True Art of Angling by J.S.
Note: Samuel Pepys' Diary, 1667, mentions "a gut string varnished over which is beyond any hair for strength and smallness. A new angling secret which I like mightily". A reference to "minikin" is probably cat-gut.
Angler's Vade Mecum by James Chetham, whose "Horseleech Fly" is the first salmon fly to receive a special name (1681). A century later this fly earns an article by Richard Brookes. Obviously a killer. Has anyone got a specimen?

18th Century

The poets Pope, Gray and Thomson, mention angling.
1746   Richard Bowlker wrote about **The Kings Fisher or Peacock Fly**. What a lure it must have been.
1786   **The North Country Angler** describes a dressing for a double-winged salmon fly. Evidently the first biplane.

19th Century

1808   **Driffield Angler** describes Macintosh's "Black Dog". Macintosh caught a salmon of 54½ lbs on this fly at Castle Menzies on the Tay.

1828 **Salmonia** by Sir Humphrey Davy, inventor of the miner's lamp. This book deals with fishing in the Highlands and observes that the best hooks were made by O'Shaughnessy of Limerick. Hooks made in London were apt to break or bend. Characteristically, Davy's book was reviewed in **The Quarterly** by a Scotsman – the author Sir Walter Scott.

1843 **Days and Nights of Salmon Fishing** by William Scrope. More quoted than any book of the period and not just because he describes flies used on the Tweed, in particular the inventions of Hames Wright of Sprouston (near Kelso) – Silver Grey, Durham Ranger, Thunder and Lightning, Silver, Black and Blue Doctors, Dandy and White Wing.

1867 **Book on Angling** by Francis Francis gives 235 patterns of salmon flies, whereas in the 1887 publication of **Salmon and Trout** only twenty-one patterns are quoted.

1895 **The Salmon Fly** by Kelson. This enterprising mass-producer claims 250 patterns, many of which were the creations of predecessors, notably Hames Wright.

Encyclopaedia Britannica, 1911, states that "Salmon fishing may be said to have become a pastime of the rich"!
The earliest Fishing Clubs in London were:–
The True Waltonian
The Piscatorial
The Friendly Anglers
The Gresham
The Flyfishers Club.

Reeling-Up

If you are as bewildered as I am by the vast store of books on fishing, in medieval and contemporary English, in ancient Greek, Latin, French, German, Dutch, Flemish, Norwegian and Swedish, amounting to some 3,000 from AD 169 to 1982, you may possibly qualify for admittance to Broadmoor. That is, if you should attempt to read them all.

A wiser course may be to select just a few which will bring you peace, contentment and sound advice. Striving for superiority has no place in fishing for Atlantic Salmon.

2

SOME OF THE GREAT SALMON FISHERS

The names which follow are by no means comprehensive. They are known to the author as outstanding fly-fishermen for Atlantic Salmon, either from history, by the testimony of fellow anglers or by personal observation.

The list is obviously expandable. Maybe there are serious omissions. Should you, the reader, feel that an injustice has been done to a supreme performer, please send me, c/o Debrett's, names and supporting data. Fly-fishers will still be accorded the higher accolade.

J.W.C.

H.M. QUEEN ELIZABETH THE QUEEN MOTHER

Miss Beamish's employer, Mr Thornton ("The one that got away")

The Bishop of Bristol ("Night with a Salmon 1868")

The Earl of Home (69¾ lb Tweed Salmon – 1812)

P.D. Malloch ("Life History of the Salmon" – 1912)

Alexander Grant ("Fine and Far Off" by 'Jock Scott')

Arthur Wood of Cairnton ("Greased Line Fishing" by Jock Scott)

Lady Evelyn Cotterell ("Salmon Fishing on the Spey")

Mrs Jessie Tyser (the Brora)

George McCorquodale of Tulchan Lodge (Spey and Helmsdale 1891-1926)

Lt Col Cyril Heber-Percy D.S.O., MC.

Willie Matheson of the Beauly, Invernesshire, head ghillie for over 50 years to successive Lord Lovats

Earl Grey of Fallodon (Fallodon Papers)

Graesser of the Cassley, Sutherland

W. Huntington of the Awe

Miss Jessie Ballantine, holder of the British record, 64 lb Tay Salmon

Richard Waddington (Don, Dee and Deveron)

Sir Ian Walker-Okeover, Bart

Sir Julian Paget, Bart

Norway	William Bromley-Davenport on the Rauma
	Cyril Mowbray Wells, 1926-1950 on the Boldstad
	Nicholas Denissoff on the Aäro, 1894-1940
	The Duke of Westminster ("Bendor"), 1913-28 on the Alta
	The Duke of Roxburghe ("Bobo"), 1913-28 on the Alta
	Viscount Coke (4th Earl of Leicester), 1913-28 on the Alta
	Sir Henry Seton-Kerr, Bart
	The Countess of Rothes on the Eira
	Alfred Denison of Ossington (the rare fishing book collector)
Ireland	The Duke of Devonshire (grandfather of Andrew, present Duke)
	Mr W.G. Jameson at Careysville (R. Blackwater)
	Judge Kingsmill-Moore of the Slaney
	Billie Flynn of Careysville (R. Blackwater)
	John O'Brien of Careysville (R. Blackwater)
England & Wales	Miss Doreen Davey (59½ lb Wye salmon)
	J. Arthur Hutton (author of *Wye Salmon*)
	Robert Pashley ("Wizard of the Wye")
	William Senior
	H.A. Gilbert
	Lionel Sweet

Canada & U.S.A.	George La Branche (pioneer of dry fly for salmon)
	E.R. Hewitt
	Lee Wulff
	The Marquess of Lansdowne (The Grand Cascapedia)
	The Hon Victor Stanley (The Grand Cascapedia 1892)
	Joe Hubert (author)
	Dean Sage (author)
	Shirley Woods (author)
	Colonel Joseph Bates Jnr (author)
Everywhere	Ernest Crosfield
	Francis Francis
	Charles Ritz
	John Rennie
	James J. Hardy
	Major the Hon John Ashley Cooper
	John Bickerdyke
	Arthur Oglesby
	Hugh Falkus
	Col E. Drury, DSO, MC
	Major Peter Clay of Brockhampton
	The Duke of Beaufort ("Master")
	The Hon Aylmer Tryon
	Capt W. Corbett
	Ian Wood (former editor *Trout & Salmon*)
	The Lord Hollenden ("Geoffrey")
	W.G. Milne